For Alice & I
Two of the greatest I
in my life —
John + Renee Woronuk.

# QUEST
## FOR EDEN

BY
JOHN I. WORONUK

 **FriesenPress**

Suite 300 – 990 Fort Street
Victoria, BC, Canada V8V 3K2
www.friesenpress.com

**ISBN**
978-1-4602-4774-7 (Hardcover)
978-1-4602-4775-4 (Paperback)
978-1-4602-4776-1 (eBook)

*1. Biography & Autobiography, People of Color*

Distributed to the trade by The Ingram Book Company

A historical novel of four Ukrainian-Canadian families whose tenacity opened a portion of Alberta's Peace River Country to cereal grain production. Their migration over a virtually impassible Edson-Grande Prairie trail a century ago initiated a massive settlement that made this unique portion of Northern Alberta an agricultural haven for this industry. Their dedication and effort represent the kind of substance that typified Canadians of various ethnic backgrounds that built the nation we cherish today.

# ACKNOWLEDGMENTS

T o credit the many people who supported me, in such various and effective ways in writing this manuscript, is one of the great pleasures of writing. First, I acknowledge the love and patience of my wife, Lorena, and her endurance in correcting count-less errors and providing guidance from her extensive research into the genealogy of my family. Without her, the first word would never have been written. Then there are my sons, Nick, Dave and Doug and their wives, Sharon, Diane and Lisa, who's gentle prompting was like a tonic.

I am deeply indebted to my niece, Claire Powell and dear friend Norma Hill, methodical editors, who brightened the manuscript using their extensive experience and academic background,. To my pub-lisher, FriesenPress, and particularly my book manager Jody Hagel, for the support I was given throughout the publishing process, I express my sincerest appreciation.

Dr. Brian Arthur Brown, and his delightful wife Jenny, it was their encouragement that prompted me to explore the joy or writing. Dr.

Ralph Clarke for methodically pushing just a little to make it happen. To all the friends in the complex in which we live: Margaret and Chris Cavacuiti, Anna Bach and her sister Marg Anderson, Doug and Shannon Grant, and all the others that join us for coffee on Wednesday mornings. Your interest has been the fuel that helped me keep going along the way.

I offer special thank you to my granddaughter Heather Woronuk, for using her skills for the map illustrations and to my cousin Igor Woroniuk for providing his immense artistic virtuosity to the cover and the illustrations that introduce each part in the book.

I express my thanks to Kelly and Brian Woronuk, my nephews, who initiated and organized the Homestead 100 celebration, that brought so many of us together and helped source some of the material in this book. Because of each of you I have enjoyed months of challenging and joyful involvement that otherwise I may never have experienced.

John Woronuk

July 2014

# FOREWORD

John Woronuk writes a northern Canadian wilderness epic in a Joseph Conrad style, concerning events that unfolded at the very time Conrad was writing about challenges in the wilds of Africa. Woronuk gets us to the soul of Canada in a manner not unlike Conrad who gets us into other emerging cultures. Both have roots in the current Ukrainian nation that did not exist when Conrad left Berdichev, where he was born in 1857, near where the first characters in this story were born a dozen years later. When Conrad describes the material world and physical actions, they are always related to psychology and motivation. The main difference is that Conrad writes international fiction whereas Woronuk recounts a true and recurrent Canadian story. Just as Conrad's journey into Africa is really a journey into the human heart, Woronuk's trek into the Canadian wilderness is an expedition to the soul of Canada, written just in time for the one hundred and fiftieth anniversary of our country's birth as a nation. It will move many who know the challenges our ancestors endured, and serve as an inspiration to new Canadians today who face great difficulties of their own.

Leaving the village of Rycroft in Northern Alberta in his teens, John Woronuk completed high school in Edmonton followed by programs and a doctorate degree after attending three American universities, Stanford, University of Washington, and The Health Sciences University of Oregon and the University of Alberta in Canada. He graduated as a Doctor of Dental Medicine in 1957 and came home, wedded to Lorena, the love of his life, to whom he has been married for 58 years as this book appears in print. They moved to Dawson Creek in Northern British Columbia, across the Alberta border from Rycroft, sharing the challenges of professional, family, church and community life. John was elected to the American Academy of Restorative Dentistry and presented at its Chicago meeting on "Fixed Prosthodontics," which I think has something to do with my gold fillings that are still in place over forty years later. He succeeded me in the Chair of the Board of Governors of the four campus Northern Lights Community College, and took an extra M.Sc. at the University of Alberta while teaching there after retirement from his dental practice. Now in another "retirement" in Kelowna, BC, he is emerging as an exceptional author with this gem of a book, dazzling in its brilliance.

The book has a subtext of tart religious flavour when John's father, Nick Woronuk, rejects the exclusivism of the Orthodox tradition on the frontier. He was determined to express a deeply rooted faith in concert with neighbours of other traditions. The United Church of Canada was born out of such pioneer sentiments, becoming a Canadian standard brand religion, and the Woronuk patriarch especially liked that "United" name. Pretty well all the Lazoruks, Chalus' and Woronuks of this story, like many others in the Ukrainian community, made the United Church of Canada their default religion, in part due to the work of a dozen or so priests who left Orthodox Orders in Winnipeg in 1910 for this same reason, becoming Presbyterian briefly *en route* to the United Church union in 1925. As a minister, most of my western and northern congregations were Ukrainian in majority, and in Dawson Creek, BC, my dentist was also the community's leading musician. So I asked John Woronuk to direct the music program at our church. He said, "No, Brian, I don't need the criticism I would face from an audience like our congregation." I replied, "No, John, your Orthodox forbearers would insist that congregations are not audiences. God is the audience." There was a long pause before John spoke: "I never thought of it that way. I'm sorry. Now I cannot refuse. With deepest humility, I do accept the position." And for several years the congregation was treated to Antonin Dvorak, Rimsky Korsakov and moving Slavonic musical support for the liturgy. With the collapse of the Soviet Union, and with new found generosity of spirit, the Orthodox Churches are today among the fastest growing religious denominations in North America, and both John and I are delighted to see the Ukrainian Orthodox Church of Canada as part of the vanguard. In a hundred years, life has come full circle. The universe is unfolding as it should, and this magnificent book is the evidence of what people with determination and faith can do.

With profound pleasure I recall long conversations in Dawson Creek at my residence, his farmhouse, the Old Vienna and Black Lantern restaurants, with wives Jenny and Lorena, debating right and left wing political idealism in the Canadian context. John had "Social Credit" views, which to me seemed like a Canadian precursor of the American Tea Party; he regarded my New Democratic "socialism" as too much akin to communism. So I was delighted to see the balance he struck in this book between the failure of Soviet communism and the opportunity presented to hard working immigrant families in Canada by Western capitalism — though I would still remind him of the government's program of homesteading in which his family got its start. Amazingly those earlier conversations were never heated, each tolerantly attempting to assist the other to see the light before returning to typical Canadian life in the moderate middle as we went to work each day, served in church and community, caring for and supporting our families in a basically identical pattern.

Readers will catch the tenor of this man's flair and style from his email to me upon his reading the first draft of these remarks. "Brian, I thought we had settled that business years ago at the Black Lantern just before midnight one dark, dank and dismal night with the wind howling, the western windows rattling, and the lights of the restaurant blinking, warning that we should be at home. There was nothing benevolent in the Homestead Act in the US and similarly nothing benevolent in Canada. The outstretched hand to Eastern Europeans of Slavic background was not offered as a social good for this distressed population to come to Canada to better themselves. It was to assure a return on investment to railway magnates. The original deal offered 20 miles of land on each side of the track to the railway investors to sell to the destitute settler at whatever price they could negotiate. Homesteads were to begin after that corridor. That didn't work. Settlers were broke and transportation to the railway was impractical. They reduced that to a narrow strip but only after the original plan flopped. Still grain farmers wouldn't come and it was then that they appealed to the Slavs to come. These were so poor that even the hopeless agricultural land of the Canadian Shield was gobbled up. I credit my dad with the vision to take a chance in the Peace Country and I credit my mother, uncles and aunts with the courage they had to follow this wild wise man. Now don't I sound like a Socialist? That's why I enjoyed you and Jenny so much. After each debate I think I ended up taking your side somehow.

Skullduggery! But you are right…whatever the reason for the offering of free land, it was right for its time and right for all of us who "capitalized" (or is it 'socialized") because of it."

# Brian Arthur Brown

(Brown is the editor of the book, *Three Testaments: Torah, Gospel & Quran* and one of the authors of the commentary in that volume as yet another wave of seemingly strange folk seek to find their way into mainstream North American life.)

# QUEST FOR EDEN

The story of four young families whose unrelenting toil
was rewarded by a land they equated to Eden

# PREFACE

*I can hear their voices...*

*I can see their faces...*

*They're all sitting around the kitchen table: Nick and Maria; Mike and Domka; Steve and Elana; visiting with my dad, Nick, while my mom, Erena, prepares food.*

*Food; there's always food. No one enters this house without being fed. Maybe it's because each of them have known hunger and know the value of food over any other commodity. To them, food is wealth, not the black numbers on a spreadsheet. Mom won't even bake brown bread, for example. She says she's eaten enough "dark" bread and rabbit and partridge. "We were poor then," she says, "but now we eat white bread." I guessed that white was rich and dark was not. All that could be white, and still practical, is white, or near so: the walls, ceiling, and kitchen tabletop cover. I think I'm living in the White House; and in winter, not only the house, the whole country is white.*

*Each of these four families thinks alike. They don't talk about the money they have in the bank or stashed away somewhere in the yard in a sealed coffee can, but how the crop did last fall, how the garden would grow in the spring, and how the kids are doing in school. It is during this kind of reflection on the past, present, and the future that mom stacks a tray with doughnuts dipped in white icing sugar and pours black coffee into white cups…but then quickly doctors it with farm cream and white sugar and morphs it more white than black.*

*The table is in a constant flux: the number sitting around it changes: Elana, Maria and Domka rise up from their chairs each time mom is about to do something in which they might help. At one time, all eight are sitting in an oblong circle, like us kids around a game of marbles, and in the next moment there are only four men — the women have left, sugaring more doughnuts, pouring more coffee, or as mother opens a jar of preserved wild raspberries, they're setting out more dishes.*

*Dad leaves the table to go downstairs to stoke the furnace with another log or two, and heat starts to rise from a register on the floor. There is no fan to move the air around — no electricity to turn it. Whoever sits nearest the register enjoys the heat it provides to his back, just like whoever sits across the table nearest Erena's cook stove.*

*An Aladdin lamp, its ornate yellow glass bowl near filled with kerosene, the mantle gleaming white, sits near the middle of the table, and the shadows of the occupants stretch from the light, like strips of dark carpet across the floor and up a wall. I find it fun to watch the shadows, listen to the conversation, and guess who is talking by watching the movements of the speaker's jaw from the shadow alone.*

*There is no extra kitchen chair for me. This is an adult night; kids are welcome to listen and somehow we get the message that our input would be interruptive. When we're old enough to take over the farm, there will be another chair at the table. Before that, we listen or leave the room, and no one notices one way or the other.*

*That's not quite true. Mom knows. Don't ask me how. Somehow, participating in the conversation, busy at the stove, she can tell you exactly where each of her sons are at any given moment. It's uncanny!*

*The guests are all comfortable and effusive; sometimes several are talking at once, and there is spontaneous laughter or sudden silence when something sad is brought up. Then men resort to short coughs and swallows to loosen their choking throats, giving away that they too are tortured by emotion. The women wipe their eyes with the hems of their aprons or reach down into the cleavage of their breasts and extract a handkerchief. The subject is left unresolved, like an unfinished painting, pushed aside until a new wave of inspiration moves the artist. Little by little the conversation returns to normal.*

*This evening is a rare occasion: Steve and Elana Chalus have come. They don't visit others much; there aren't enough hours in the day to do the work Steve commits to himself and Elana. What an opportunity for them, to be together, to reflect on their common experiences, to chuckle about the near misses, to gasp or weep at some of them, to recollect a period of their lives when they had been young, strong, foolhardy — or had they been brilliant?*

*It's special for me. I am Nick and Erena's youngest son, and this occasion has been in my mind's eye since the evening itself over seven decades ago.*

*I need to tell the story of this event, coupled to many others that occurred, but with fewer participants. These eight were the adults of four families who braved following a trail some 350 miles to settle on rock-free black soil, rich in nutrients, which they could clear and till, and from which they might prosper. It was a discussion that recalled hope, but even more than the word hope implies; it was a faith, so strong, so focused, that all the elements that stacked against them could not shatter it.*

*This is a Canadian story: a struggle to locate on the northern periphery of a part of this country's massive expanse of land where cereal grains could still grow. It is a story of courage that bore these families through toil, tears, and joy. Families who wed in order to build on a dream, believing love would blossom only as the dream materialized. Some depended on the constancy that their religious spirit provided; in others, religion was diluted, but their steadfastness was reconstituted by elements of their own internal spirit.*

*They had their dreams, and Canada had her dreams too. A free people of a new Canadian nation watched in horror as its neighbor to the south, the United States, unfurled as a fledgling republic from its War of Independence. More wars followed, and it finally burst into a drastic Civil War that bled its North and decimated its South.*

*Canada shuddered as the new Republic's euphoria threatened to absorb the western part of a huge North American landmass of unclaimed territory. Rail transportation and settlement were the key essentials to preserve the western objectives of the recent Dominion status that Canada had been granted.*

*If settlers could create produce, the railways would distribute it. To fill the former, Canada opened its doors to immigrants from Eastern Europe in the late 1880s. The eastern extension of the Austro-Hungarian Empire was teeming with would-be farmers, and their land could not sustain the growing population. Migration to Canada was an opportunity; the Dominion Lands Act that offered free land as homesteads created a bonanza.*

*Some of the Chalus, Lazoruk, and Woronuk families emigrated from Bukovina, Austria, to the Stuartburn district in Manitoba. Steve and Elana (nee Lazoruk) Chalus, Nick and Maria (nee Korol) Lazoruk, Mike and Domka (nee Rosko) Lazoruk, and Nick and Erena (nee Lazoruk) Woronuk, as immigrants, were directed by Canadian authorities to settle on the rocky western border of the Canadian Shield, in southeastern Manitoba. They disengaged themselves from that impossible agricultural environment, and chose to move to the northwestern part of Alberta to stake their claims on productive soil, with hopes for a better future. The year was 1913.*

*I write this in 2013. On July 1, the farmsteads north of the village of Rycroft hosted a 100th Anniversary celebration of the arrival of these four families, the first dedicated cereal grain producers in the Rycroft area. One hundred seventy-five direct descendants from Canada, United States, and England attended. Like the kitchen table discussion at the Woronuk family home over seventy years ago, multiplied some twenty times in terms of the numbers present, stories that were related by mothers, fathers, grandmothers and grandfathers pervaded those two days and nights of celebration.*

*Over seventy years ago, when I was thirteen years old, I had listened to that kitchen discussion, and at this gathering, I was listening again. The same sense of captivation moved me on each of these occasions. The "back-then" was filed in a youngster's memory to be recalled in snippets now and again as conversations dictated, but the "now" forced a sense of urgency to record in print the events that so fascinated me. This writing connects the experiences in the lives of these remarkable Canadians whose tenacity helped build the country that they adopted, unequivocally, as home.*

# PART I

# CHAPTER 1

Nick," Mike Lazoruk pointed his finger at Nick Woronuk, "you came to our place back in 1911 to court my sister Erena." There is a twinkle in Mike's eye. Nick has been his best friend from that time, and the question is clearly loaded. "What was it you were you looking for?"

Erena broke into the discussion, "Yes, tell him, Nick. I was afraid you were going to ask my dad for my hand in marriage, and I wanted to run away. You were cute, but I was just sixteen. I suspected what it was you had in mind!"

There was laughter, and Nick, with that captivating smile that would characterize him all his life, winked at Mike and replied, "I was looking to make an investment. You knew I had made some money. I had to find someone to help me spend it. Your sister was a real help in that regard!"

They chuckled. They knew Erena to be frugal, not to the extent that Nick was, but careful with every cent. They all were. Frugality assured a road to survival. Hard work paved it.

Steve, still laughing, reminded Erena that when he asked for her sister Elana's hand in marriage, he wore work clothes, not a suit and hat like Nick did. "You see," he said, "how quickly times had changed."

"I had to go across the line to Minnesota to find Maria," Nick Lazoruk admitted. "There was no one in Arbakka as suitable as she, so I brought her over the border. You talk about an investment, Nick; man, did I capitalize! She's given me thirteen kids! Much of the time I get their names mixed up."

"Domka uses her own mind, but my money," Mike quipped. "How rich would I be if I didn't make my investment with the Rosko family?"

Domka punched Mike on the shoulder. "You lucky dog," she said. "You would have starved or died from fleas and lice if it wasn't for one bright moment in your entire life, when you asked my dad for me."

It was good-natured banter, but as the evening progressed, it evolved into a recollection of events that would live even more vividly in my memory. What I would give today, to have the chance to review those events with those who told them! But they have all passed on. I am alone with my memories, the last living in the Woronuk family as a first generation descendant of Nick and Erena.

The world had changed for those around the table that winter evening at the Woronuk home. They were once *oxeneers*, men who knew how to train and drive oxen. Nick Lazoruk, alone, had experience with horses, and the transition to horses as draft animals was initiated by him, and then followed by the others. Replacing oxen with horses was the first upgrading of their farming operations.

At the time that this get-together occurred, a second major change was taking place: they were buying motorized equipment that none at the table could learn to operate. Each had sons who could, and did, and through their sons, each farm kept pace with modernization. Now

in the comfort of a warm room, with sugared doughnuts and sweet-
ened coffee, they reminisced.

# CHAPTER 2

I didn't sleep well that night. The stories I heard from around that table kept racing through my mind, and I tried to imagine myself in the shoes of the storyteller. It's not easy for a kid to do, and it left my stomach churning, wondering if I would ever grow to be made of stuff like my mom and dad. Morning came, and it was Sunday: no school. I wanted to ask Dad the questions that I wouldn't the night before, with the other adults present.

Dad came in from his chores outside and sat in his regular place, to the side of the cook stove where it was warmest. Mother was making breakfast, and she poured him a cup of coffee, adding cream and sugar while he held the cup out in front of him. Now over 50-years-old, he'd been to the barn to feed six cattle and five horses before he himself was fed. He would have to go back and lead each team of horses to water, then drive the cattle to the trough, and dip water out of a dugout, one that he had dug and lined its walls with logs. A coal oil lantern would light his way.

In this country, the sun, in the heart of winter, rises after 9 a.m. and sets by 4 p.m. And it is cold. It can reach -60 F. It was not that cold on this morning, but it was cold enough. The heat in the kitchen was from mother's Huron cook stove, a beautiful kitchen appliance of chrome on black, with two ovens faced with white *porcelain. Mother had a roaring fire going in the firebox, and she had opened the lower oven door to allow its heat to escape into the kitchen.*

"Dad," I asked, "how did you learn to speak English?" I heard my own question and immediately felt embarrassed by it. I had thought of a hundred questions to ask, and then started with the most unfitting one of all. In retrospect, any question I could have asked would have seemed equally inappropriate. Somehow, through the previous years, the only questions that I had asked of my father had been related to things about myself, when I needed his guidance. Now I was asking about him, for the first time, and for some reason, it sounded presumptuous.

"I'm sorry," I added quickly, "That was a dumb question." By now I was flustered, and felt the heat of embarrassment crawl up my neck and face.

"No son," he interrupted, "it's a good question." He saw my flushed face and may have felt sorry for me. He went on to tell me about his life. It didn't take that day, or that week, it took years. A little anecdote here, another there, and slowly my mind built a library of his experiences.

As these events accumulated, my interests sometimes waned. I turned 14, 15, and then 16, and I suffered the maturation problems of any normal boy. During some of those stories, I rebelled enough to question the judgments of the group. I was ashamed of my background. I wanted to be the son of a noble, a duke or something, and be able to go to school proud and respected, rather than be the son of immigrant parents.

I was more open with my mother. It was she who set me straight when I began to ramble about the lack of good sense (in the opinion of a 13-year-old) that had occurred on events decades before I was born. Her dark brown eyes would flash, and she would respond before I had reached the central point in my argument. She had raised four sons before me, knew this stage well, and once said, "Some of the best wild strawberries are those that choose to grow in the worst of weeds."

Dad told me about his English learning. It might have started with *Once upon a time*, but he didn't use that phrase. He introduced me to more than his English learning; he introduced me to himself.

My dad, Nicholas, began by telling me about his first winter in Canada, working in a lumber camp as a tree faller, near Winnipeg, Manitoba. Another worker with him asked:

"Who are you, Nicholas?

The camp boss says you are Austrian, but you speak a language that does not in any way resemble German. You wear a sheepskin coat and a fur hat; you're tough as nails but generous to a fault. You can't be much more than 5½ feet tall, but your character should fit someone twice your size.

Once again, who are you Nicholas?"

Nicholas shouldered his axe and turned to face his prober. His mind raced through the questions, but no answer seemed fitting. He had never before been asked to respond to such a simple question that was so difficult to answer. Even coming through emigration in Trieste, or the immigration line at Ellis Island in New York, not even at the border crossing into Canada, did anyone ask who he was. It was all on paper, on his ship's document: he was Nicholaj Waroinuk, from Onut, Bukovina, in the Austrian Empire. He was immigrating to Canada to start a new life with the promise of land, lots of land, not just a share of a single acre that his father would subdivide between him and his older brother, Simon. Neither would have had enough for a decent garden.

Who am I? Nicholas pondered. That is a good question! In 1906 I am an Austrian. But I speak Ukrainian, and my sheepskin coat is warmer than your mackinaw. I am much smaller than you, but I can cut trees all day without showing fatigue, and you have to sit and rest nearly every hour. Yes, I shared my lunch with you because you didn't have enough to feed your large frame, and I smiled when I did it. I didn't realize that this simple act would impress you, and you would then judge my character from that gesture alone. But your compliment, along with the question from you, an English speaking person, to an immigrant with just enough English vocabulary to vaguely understand what you asked; that is surprising.

"Stanley, I try answer you. I be Nickolai Voronyouk. Very poor English, sorry. I in Canada maybe six months and I be 17 years old. Immigration write Waroinuk, so I be Nicholaj Waroinuk, ok? But English call me Nicholas Woronuk. So now I Nicholas Woronuk," he chuckles. "I not so strong like you say, but I sharpen axe every few trees. You rest, I sharpen; you rest again, I sharpen again. One cut better than your two. I show you, ok?"

Nicholas took Stanley's axe and carefully examined its cutting edge. He drew his thumbnail across its edge. Little spurs caught his nail; the edge was neither sharp nor efficient. With old country skill, he stoned Stanley's axe. The barbs disappeared, and the edge glistened and flashed like snow crystals in winter sunlight. It took a few minutes before he handed the axe back. Stanley drew the blade across his hairy forearm, and some hair shaved off. He shook his head. "This axe has never been this sharp."

To say a thank you might have emasculated a woodsman's character, but a look of admiration and respect was better suited. Stanley gazed a moment at the axe edge, then turned to face Nicholas. He nodded slightly, rose up, and took the steps to the next poplar. The first slightly upward horizontal stroke sunk the blade deep into the body of the trunk. The second stroke, some ten inches above the first and angled to the ground, peeled off a substantial wedge of wood and sent it spinning away several feet from the tree. Two more such cuts would suffice, followed by one on the opposite side, and a push toppled the tree. Five or six swings of the axe and one push, and the tree was down — unbelievable, the effort — minimal. Who is this Nicholas?

A few trees later, Nicholas stopped Stanley and reached for his axe. With a little hesitation, Stanley handed it over. Nicholas probed his back pocket and pulled out the stone. Two or three gentle strokes and he returned the axe to the hulking Stanley. Several strikes later, another tree had fallen, but as if in its place, a friendship was sprouting. Pay was two cents per tree for falling and another three cents for trimming, and Stanley could now keep pace with the proportionately diminutive Nicholas.

After the sun had set behind the western horizon of southeastern Manitoba, each woodsman had earned well over a dollar — a good day. They struck up an agreement: "I keep axe sharp, Stanley; you teach me English."

As darkness was descending, Stanley followed a road in the direction to the lumber camp on whose lease they were working. Nicholas turned the opposite way. Stanley asked him where he was going. "To uncle place," Nicholas replied.

"Oh, does your uncle live near here?" Stanley asked.

"Not far, seventeen kilometers," Nicholas replied, still using the metric system from Austria.

"My God," exclaimed Stanley. "You are walking. That's about 10 miles, after a whole day's work? Why?"

"Save money. Uncle place cheaper. Need money to send to Austria for family."

Stanley shook his head in bewilderment. They had started cutting at first light, at 7:00 in the morning. It was now 12 hours later and this youngster was going to walk 10 miles to save a few cents. *He's going to walk back in darkness in the morning. What is he made of anyway?*

Nicholas set a fast pace, just under a jog, but it didn't seem to tire him. Down the road a bit he began to whistle, a skill well developed before he left his homeland. So much so, in fact, that on the way to school in Onut, Jewish store owners would stop him and request he whistle particular Jewish themes, especially a Kuchen, which he could embellish with grace notes and brief trills; yet he always maintained a strict rhythm. His listeners would clap and stomp their feet, and then compensate him with a piece of white bread. White bread! A delicacy unseen in a peasant household: rare, like caviar on this continent.

Oh, Nicholas could whistle! His pace matched the rhythm, and time seemed to fly by. In less than three hours he was at his uncle's place. It was a shack, near Stuartburn, a small village between Winnipeg and the American border, where the state of Minnesota meets the province of Manitoba.

When Nicholas arrived, Uncle John was up, sitting on the bench at the table in the one room cabin that was lit only by the flame from a homemade oil lamp. Aunt Sanchera had left boiled potatoes and salt pork for Nicholas, and hot water was on the pot-bellied stove in the center of the room from which to make fresh tea. Minimal fare following a hard day's work, but Nicholas did not complain. He was in Canada, he was free to work, to make money, to one day own land like Uncle John, to build a cabin, and have a family. Prodigious dreams these were, for a seventeen-year-old.

"You tired?" Uncle John asked.

"Stiff, a little. More hungry and thirsty than tired," Nicholas replied. "But it was a good day. I made a dollar for cutting and another dollar for trimming some of the trees I had cut."

"You will soon be a rich man," his uncle teased. "Then you will marry and have a fat wife and eat white bread."

They both laughed at the image John crafted. Nicholas's thoughts about marriage were fleeting. Girls were interesting, but they took a back seat to making money. Money: something that came in coins and in paper, and the paper form was something he had first held in his hands when he was leaving Austria for Canada.

His bed, in one corner of the cabin, was constructed from willow boughs covered with moss to level the sleeping surface. The cover was a collection of dried rabbit skins, roughly sewn together with strips of leather. In summer and winter it was infested with fleas; the rabbit hides were simply salted and dried, but not tanned. Although the salt discouraged reproduction of these pests, it alone was never a major barrier to infestation. When Nicholas lay in bed, and his body warmed the space around him, the fleas would awaken from their dormancy in winter, and begin a feeding frenzy on any exposed skin.

Around four in the morning, Nicholas arose and prepared a breakfast of ground wheat and barley, boiled in water to make porridge. There was no sugar, but salt would substitute as a taste enhancer. For lunch, he prepared a couple slices of dark bread lathered with fat that Aunt Sanchera had carefully saved from cooking. She stored it in an earthen jar placed on the floor near the door to cool and stiffen. From another jar, he took dill pickles, and from yet another, some sauerkraut, and this morning, a little extra in case Stanley needed some. These he placed it in an empty syrup can and was back on the trail to his work site.

The eastern horizon was beginning to show a streak of crimson in preparation for the rising sun, but in the forest, the darkness was like ink. The snow contrasted with the stumps from cut timber, and Nicholas's eyes, now adjusted to the dark, helped him avoid tripping over countless snags that protruded like trapper's snares across his trail. Occasionally, a ruffed grouse would burst from its slumber, fracturing the night's silence like breaking glass. The rest was stillness, except for the rhythmic crush of snow beneath his feet.

Nicholas located his axe, driven into a stump of a tree that he'd cut the day before. He reached into his pocket for the stone he had brought from Onut: a grey flattened piece of fine volcanic rock, found rarely along the banks of the Dniester River. The finder treasured such a stone much as a woman would treasure a jeweled necklace. A few gentle strokes along the cutting edge and another workday would begin.

Later, the sun now lighting the horizon, Stanley could hear the hefts of a tree cutter in the distance. *Surely this kid has not already walked 10 miles and began cutting before I have even arrived*, he thought. But the rhythm of the strokes was unmistakable; it was, indeed, Nicholas. They greeted each other briefly; Stanley could not help but notice that at least five new trees lay denuded of their branches and ready to be dragged to the mill, a mile away. This was going to be a profitable day for Nicholas — the early start was like a bonus on top of his day's earnings.

As Stanley withdrew his axe from an adjacent stump, Nicholas came over holding his stone. Nicholas trued its cutting edge as he reminded Stanley of the pact they had made the day before: "Teach me English, and I sharpen axe." So began a winter's course in verbal English in the forests of southeastern Manitoba, between an English speaking woods-man and a peasant Austro-Ukrainian.

# CHAPTER 3

*R*emarkable story," I thought. And then I did something voluntarily that I have no memory of doing before. While Dad was finishing breakfast, I put on my winter boots and mackinaw to accompany him to the barn to assist with chores. It was an unconscious action that surprised me, and, I'm sure, shocked him. Like most teenagers, I did what was assigned to me, but volunteer? Never! It was clear I wanted to hear more, and by today's definition, my dad and I were bonding. Bill, my second oldest brother, destined to be the farmer that would inherit an extra chair at the table one day, walked with us to the barn, and Dad continued:

"My father, George Woronuk, had emigrated from Austria in 1904 when I was fourteen," Dad said as we followed him in line along the tramped snow pathway to the barn. "He followed his two married daughters, your aunts, who made the passage to Canada in 1903, and left the remaining family of two daughters and two sons, which included me, and your grandmother, in Onut."

My mother later filled in what Dad had left unsaid. Dad's precociousness, his vibrant personality, and his musical skills made him a favorite in the family and in the village. Working in jobs that were available in Canada and the United States, Grandfather George was saving every penny in order to bring the rest of his family to Canada. The first was to be his son, Nicholas.

I learned that the letters from my Grandfather George and Dad's older married sisters spoke of the wonders of opportunity that their adopted country offered. The gift of land — free — as a homestead, through the Dominion Lands Act, required only the payment of a registration fee. This was a plot of land a half mile square, containing 160 acres, the equivalent of significant wealth in homeland Austria. Each male 18 years of age or older was eligible to apply. If the homestead was improved sufficiently after a few years, the homesteader would be given a title of full ownership to the land.

Such opportunity was unimaginable in crowded Bukovina. Landowners of wealth were officers and friends of the Austrian courts, rewarded by gifting them with ownership of land as compensation for their exemplary military services or other service to the Kaiser, Franz Joseph of the Habsburgs. The population was primarily peasants. Outside of compulsory military service at age 21, there was freedom, but little opportunity to raise oneself from the peasant class.

Dad, along with every young man in the community, knew this, so when this condition was coupled with the mass advertising of what Canada was offering, the desire to emigrate was rampant amongst the young men. But Nicholas's yearning bordered on the irrational. He understood his mother's love for him, and he conceived an adolescent plan to make his departure more tolerable. He told his mother that he would so aggravate his younger sisters, Sophia and Rose, she would be pleased to see him leave. With his alertness, he nearly succeeded. As the children rebelled to his incessant teasing, his mother once pleaded,

"Don't fight back. He will soon be gone to Canada, and then we will all miss him so."

There was more meaning in those words than the words themselves expressed. Elana, prophetic and superstitious, once said, "Nicholas, when you leave, I will not be able to survive my sorrow."

Nicholas, of course, took this lightly and comforted her with well-chosen words, "Mother, don't despair. I will help Dad to save enough money to bring all of you to Canada. Then we will never be apart again." Canada was on his mind virtually all the time, and as he approached his seventeenth birthday, moving there became an obsession.

Springtime in Bukovina was a time of festivities. Onut, like other villages, celebrated village festivals in a central park where dancing, singing, and even romance took place. Nicholas, while attending one such event, noticed a group of young men gathered around an apparent promoter. Pushing his way through the men and boys, he was able to get within earshot of him and hear what he was saying. The man was promoting passage to Canada!

He was an animated Jewish travel agent, with a reasonable command of Ukrainian, and claimed to be able to find space aboard a steamship sailing to Canada in two weeks time. The point of departure was to be Trieste, a port city on the Adriatic, then part of Austria, in the expansive Austro-Hungarian Empire. Many of those surrounding him had already signed with him, paid their fare, and were listening for any further instructions before their departures.

On this warm spring evening, amidst the sound of music and laughter, and the sun setting, its warm glow of radiant energy casting long shadows from the thatched rooftops in the village, Nicholas had realized his dream coming true.

"I hurried home," Dad said, "so excited I was hardly able to talk. I told my mother the excellent news and about the rush to make preparations to leave in two weeks! I was shocked to see her burst into tears."

Nicholas had to telegram his father in Canada to immediately forward the passage money to the Jewish agent. Canada did not require passports, according to the agent, so application for that document was not necessary. Onut was, and still is a village 50 kilometers from Chernovtsi, the city from which he could take a train to the port of Trieste. The agent suggested Nicholas travel to a neighboring community and join with some adult emigrants who would provide room for him on their wagon to Chernovtsi.

"Mother now wept almost constantly. She had a beautiful voice and sang tender, sorrowful songs about losing her son to a foreign land. The Empire, she knew, offered me no hope for an improved future. I tried to assure her that with the opportunities Canada offered, we would all be together soon. Mother sewed me a bag for my possessions from the best bleached white cloth she could obtain, for neither she nor I had ever seen a suitcase."

For Nicholas it was both an exciting and sad time. His love for his mother was intense, and her tears were most difficult for him to bear. But the excitement of getting to Canada, the subject of his dreams since his father's first letters arrived two years earlier, was finally being fulfilled. It was a two-week period filled with grief one moment and joy the next. When word came that the agent had, in fact, received the money for the voyage, Nicholas then settled and adopted a stable, mature mood of anticipation.

# CHAPTER 4

Onut was a little village in the early twentieth century, a collection of peasant huts, a few storekeepers, a school and such. It differed from Canadian or American villages both in its topography and in its evolution. As a progressive step from historic serfdom, Austrian landowners were required to provide a strip of their estates to the male peasants who toiled on the landlord's holdings. As the population grew, this constant subdivision of the estate became an economic problem for the landowners. To maintain financial security, they instigated an extra burden of rent to the peasant, for the land they had provided to him.

Unable to acquire more of the landlord's estate, the peasant was forced to subdivide his own minimal allotment among his sons. Nicholas knew the consequences, as did every other young man: their futures would become more dismal than that of their parents. With annexation of Bukovina by the Austrian Empire over a century earlier, the last vestiges of serfdom were eliminated, but peasants were still economically and traditionally tied to the land. They had, however, gained freedom to leave to find better environments for their lives.

Villages like Onut developed, in part, because no peasant owned sufficient land to be separate from his neighbor by any appreciable distance. Besides, history played a part. Bukovina was situated on some of the finest agricultural land in Europe and suffered a tragic history by being overrun by hordes of invaders. People clustered in village-like groups, hoping that their cumulative numbers might act as an obstacle to the butchery that history had recorded.

In Canada in the late nineteenth century, massive railway projects were underway. The government of the day realized that this transportation mechanism was critical to the preservation of the West within Canadian Confederation. To encourage speculators, large land grants were assigned to the railway companies to encourage investment in railroad construction. But to continue to capitalize, the railways needed freight to haul, and for that to occur, land settlement and agriculture were essential.

Clifford Sifton, Minister of the Interior in the John A. MacDonald government, recognized the problem and persuaded the government to promote the immigration of farmers from Eastern Europe and the United States. The Dominion Lands Act of 1872 was modeled after the earlier Homestead Act of the United States. There it had instigated a massive western migration. With few, but significant improvements, the Dominion Lands Act became the key legislated incentive that encouraged farmer and rancher migration to Western Canada. Through it, the economic security of the railway magnates was supported as well as the national territorial aspirations of the new Dominion of Canada.

Nicholas was unaware of the politics underlying the Canadian opportunity. He only knew that free land was available for no more than a registration fee. For years before he could emigrate, Bukovinians and Galicians had been immigrating to Canada, and their letters were full of praise, hope, and success.

Some relatives had gone almost immediately when the word was out that Clifford Sifton's grand scheme to settle the West had been legislated. The exodus of young men was of concern to the Austro-Hungarian Empire, because it was cutting deeply into its source of military manpower. Service to the Kaiser was mandatory, and would entail sacrificing a minimum of two years of the most productive time of every male subject. Nicholas was very aware of the interruption to his life that the military service would create. Canada offered an escape, and it offered opportunity. It was little wonder that he was obsessed with leaving Onut.

*Dad's explanation went on following a chronological pattern with word choices that painted a picture of the events, as they unfolded, to bring him to Canada. From his vivid description, I visualized a scene that has stayed imprinted in my memory these many years.*

# CHAPTER 5

The night before his departure, Nicholas listened to the gentle sobs of his mother, neither of the two having slept. Morning came with bright sunlight spreading like a delicate breeze, catching the tips of trees, then descending to the shrubs and plants, and finally spreading, with the shadows it created, over the surface of the earth. It was too beautiful a day to be so filled with melancholy. It was too beautiful a day to be his last in Onut. It was harder to leave than Nicholas had imagined, and looking into the tear-filled tired eyes of his mother, whom he considered the most wonderful woman on earth, Nicholas too wept uncontrollably.

Through her sobs, Elana uttered comforting words of hope for success in Nicholas's life-changing adventure. She no longer attempted to change the tide of his life, but simply offered her prayers for him.

Nicholas hoisted the sack of his belongings over his shoulder and turned to walk away. A few steps later, he turned toward his mother again; she stood there weeping uncontrollably, rivulets of tears following the creases in her cheeks, across the corners of her mouth, where she interrupted their course and wiped them away. He waved, and she raised her hand — a final farewell to her beloved son. That image of his gentle mother, standing alone near the gate to his home, would remain with him for the rest of his life. He would never see her again.

Onut slowly faded in the distance. As though creating a reflection of his divided emotions, the brilliant eastern sun glowed against white-washed walls, contrasting them with their gloomy shadowed western counterparts. The road to Chornyi Potik (Black Creek), led through lush green fields of spring growth. Nicholas's pace began to pick up as the emotional trauma of the departure from his mother faded with the sight of his village, and the excitement of the future dominated his thoughts.

Occasional pangs would return: the image of his mother at the gate, her tears, an expression of a mother's grief over a son she was losing, even her own uncertain destiny, passed through his mind. He again experienced tightness, and a burning throat from his anguish, and tears welled up in his eyes. A deep breath of morning air, filled with the fragrance of pollinating plants, helped him ease the moment, and his pace would pick up again. Uncharacteristically, Nicholas did not whistle; he tried a few times but his lips would not purse.

*Dad described that when Onut was out of sight he felt his first sense of independence. "It was a sensation that coursed through my young body, down the muscles of my legs, and into my feet. It was an exhilarating feeling, like the first breath of air from a deep-water dive." His determination to make this venture an unqualified success took on an air of maturity beyond his years. Dad's imagination overflowed with images of what Canada would be like: the wonders of this remote land across an unfathomable expanse of water, with riches that he could accumulate.*

From childhood, his father, George, had taught him the skills that would serve him in Bukovina. These were basic skills that peasants would need to impress their landlords and so become valuable to them:

using a scythe, and sharpening it to perfection, sowing wheat, tying it in bundles, and threshing out the grain. He became adept at these skills, but it was his love of music that seemed to feed his soul.

With a passion hardly controllable as a child, he wanted to play a violin. His persistence persuaded his grandfather to buy him a little violin on one of his infrequent trips to Chernovtsi. The little boy, gifted with near perfect pitch, soon showed such promise that a well-regarded fiddler in a nearby community offered him instruction. Roman Bozhyk helped him with the basics of playing folk tunes, those that Nicholas had already established well in memory, and whistled with remarkable skill. Neither teacher nor student knew how to read music, but whatever skills the legendary Bozhyk had, Nicholas was soon able to mimic. Now he added his fiddling skills to that of his whistling, and the child achieved unique popularity in Onut.

One night, in the heat of summer while the family slept, a peg that kept a string taut, suddenly released. The string made a loud twang that woke most of the household. It was, as the grandfather thought, and had for some time suspected: no child could play so well without the influence of the supernatural. It was the devil that was playing, not his grandson.

The grandfather arose from his cot, brought the violin down from its peg on the wall, laid it on the floor, and with his feet, smashed it to splinters. He collected the pieces, satisfied that the first phase of ridding the family of evil was accomplished. In the dark, he took the remnants out the door to the manure compost pile. He dug deep, and uttering incantations, stuffed the wood and strings into the hole, and then covered them thoroughly. As superstition decreed, even the devil could not extricate the instrument now.

Without his violin, Nicholas's left hand often fingered the tunes on the side of his thigh. He did this now, taking brisk steps to Chornyi Potik as he soundlessly aired and fingered the familiar tunes of Bukovina.

# CHAPTER 6

The distance from Onut to Chornyi Potik was *two pipes of tobacco*, a common expression for distance in the colorful peasant dialect of Ukrainian. Nicholas found his travelling companions loading suitcases and trunks into a wagon. The two had served their time in the military and owned these unique carrying devices — so different from Nicholas's cloth sack. They welcomed him, and immediately left for Chernovtsi, from where a train would take them away from Bukovina, and deliver them to the port city of Trieste.

The horse drawn wagon with its occupants arrived in Chernovtsi the following morning. They were tired from a sleepless night, but were urged by a representative of the travel company to see the agent in his office as soon as possible. The train for Trieste was scheduled to leave at three o'clock that afternoon. The office was filled with people when they arrived, all having been similarly advised. Eventually, Nicholas was able to speak to the agent. The conversation was brief; the agent acknowledged he had received the money from Canada, and handed him the ticket for passage on the pride of Austria: the *Franz Joseph*. The great ship would be sailing directly to Canada, to either the port of Halifax or Montreal. Nicholas breathed a sigh of relief.

The agent asked Nicholas to pay for the train fare to Trieste, a sum of sixty kronen, Austrian currency of the time, and to exchange the equivalent of twenty-five dollars to Canadian to be available for costs in Canada. Nicholas pondered the rising costs against his minimal available cash. The twenty-five Canadian dollars was a concern; he had not dealt with foreign money before. Changing familiar Austrian currency to a foreign one, something called a *dollar,* was daunting, but he did it. Once done, he felt better. He sensed closeness to Canada, and with this, a new wave of alertness helped overcome his fatigue. He carefully folded the money into his waistband, separating it from the few kronen that still remained.

His companions from Chornyi Potik waited for him. Nicholas joined them, and after a few verbal exchanges, proceeded to follow the agent and the queue of men, women, and children carrying or dragging their belongings, plodding along the cobblestones to the railway station.

By 3:00 p.m., the horde, or so it seemed to a small town teenager, had found seats on the train. His seat was wooden and worn but far more comfortable than the wagon from Chornyi Potik. The engine's whistle blew, steam exploded from its boiler, and a jerk signaled that the train was in motion. Nicholas was leaving Bukovina. Unknown to him, this would be the last time that he would see this land. Yet, despite the hardships he had borne there in the past, despite the obvious lack of opportunity it offered him in the future, he experienced a period of nostalgia. His mother standing at the gate as he seemed to drift from her; his two sisters still asleep; his brother and friends he had left behind, these visions appeared before his eyes. Tears welled up and his throat burned — it was too late to reconsider.

He was not alone with his emotions. He glanced around his passenger car and noticed most women, and even some men, drying their eyes. A silence fell over the throng, with the exception of the occasional whimper from a child in need of the comfort of its familiar surroundings — its home, however simple, was no longer at hand. It was so hard to leave, Nicholas realized, but he was developing a more profound determination to prove his decision to be a wise one rather than a youthful adventure.

The train lumbered on westward, soon into the Carpathian Mountains, and then across lands other than Bukovina, the only land Nicholas had ever known. The repetitive clang of steel on steel, the monotony of motion, and the fatigue from the sleepless nights before, eventually overwhelmed him. He leaned his head against the wooden seat back and drifted into daylight sleep.

He awoke to a noisier environment with conversation, laughter, and the playful screams of children. The sadness of leaving home had begun to pass, and other passengers, like he, seemed to be coming to terms with their destiny. Some men were smoking a pungent tobacco in hand rolled cigarettes. Most were smoking curved pipes; some with the bowl top at, or even below, chin level. Pipe smoking was the custom of the time, but it left the railcar filled with smoke and its fragrance mingled with the odor of sweating bodies. No one complained, although a few windows were pried open to allow fresh air to enter.

Nicholas needed to use a washroom, but he had no idea where to find such a place in a train. His experience, both at home and at school, was with outdoors toilets, and with those he was familiar. He held on for some time hoping the train would stop, and he could find an appropriate facility to gain relief. But the train rambled on, hesitating at small villages but not permitting anyone to disembark. Finally, he asked his bench partners from Chornyi Potik how to manage his need. One chuckled at the naivety of their travelling companion, but motioned to the back of the car where there was a toilet. Nicholas saw a line of men and women waiting to access it, balancing themselves against aisle seats as the train rocked incessantly over the rails. He rose from his seat and joined the line.

A surge of water sounded from inside the enclosure—a sound like Nicholas had never heard before. Having no idea of its source, he sensed a level of anxiety. Finally, when he was next in line to enter, he heard the roar of the water again, and a few moments later a man exited from the tight space.

Nicholas's need was to urinate, fortunately, but on entry he saw an odd shaped porcelain bucket with a lid covering it. Where was the open hole to which he was accustomed? He lifted the lid and saw water in the bowl that did not run out a dark hole in the bottom.

Some of the previous sounds now began to make sense. This, he decided, was some device into which you pass your excrement and the water washes it away. Unable to procrastinate any longer, he voided. There was a cord attached to a tank above his head. He pulled the cord, and a sudden burst of water gushed into the bowl. Alarmed, Nicholas rapidly left the room, believing that the car could soon be flooded. Before his door closed, the water stopped — he had learned how to use a flush toilet!

It seems like a little thing, flushing a toilet, but to a totally uninformed peasant boy, this was tantamount to a modern spacewalk. He explained his experience to his mates back at his seat, and they chuckled goodheartedly, and then related similar humorous experiences that they had, years before, when they were first drafted into the military.

Nicholas laughed so hard at their stories that he could scarcely catch his breath. It seemed so long since the last time he had laughed…

sometime before he left Onut. To his astonishment, his lips pursed and he produced a trilling whistle. His whistling skill had returned!

Those very first sounds alerted passengers within earshot; this was no ordinary whistling skill. Heads turned, and a circle of silence occurred as those who heard the whistle realized there was extraordinary talent here. In a seat across from him, someone asked him to whistle a tune or two. He obliged, and in a minute the car grew silent as the passengers turned to hear this youngster whistle melodies they all knew. Little children left their seats to stomp their feet, wave their hands, and bend at the waist in an imperfect rhythm to his tunes.

Then a man, a few seats forward, reached above him to a luggage shelf and withdrew a mandolin. He strummed and tuned it, then joined Nicholas in the tunes they both knew. A woman with a cultured soprano voice joined in, first rather quietly, and then robustly. Hearts still grieving the departure from their homeland craved an outlet, a way to allow light to flow into the shadows created by their sorrow. In a minute the whole car was a choir, with an orchestra of a whistler and a mandolin. The conductor came through, smiled, and joined in for a moment or two. It was the beginning of a delightful trip for those in car Number 180 from Chernovtsi to Trieste.

Midway through the journey, the mountains began to recede to the east, and the verdant plains of Hungary brought back more memories of Bukovina. The towns and villages that the train passed through were now more numerous, and then the majestic city of Budapest appeared.

Wrapped around the Danube River, this city had for centuries been reputed as one of Europe's most exotic. It hosted a mosaic of Slavs, Europeans, and trading nomadic tribes from the East and the South. Budapest was a center of multiculturalism in central Europe long before that term described Canada's ethnic mosaic.

The train stopped, and passengers were allowed to disembark, stretch their legs on short walks into the city, and hear the music of outdoor Gypsy bands, music that Nicholas was so fond of and with which he was familiar. He stopped near one such group and listened to the Czardases and Horas of Gypsy lore, played by a violinist of substantial skill. Every movement of the fiddler's hands, every nuance of his skipping bow was captured, and Nicholas stored these technical skills in his mind for the day when he would once again possess a violin. His ears caught new themes, and his brain instantly memorized them, and he later whistled them on the train for the pleasure of the passengers.

On the third day, they reached the historic city of Trieste, a great port on the northern periphery of the Adriatic Sea. This city had changed its citizenship countless times over the centuries, and its architecture and its people represented the various ethnicities and cultures left behind from these transgressions. Such cultural and architectural characteristics were readily visible, but to Nicholas they were of secondary importance. He needed to find his agent, who had travelled on the train with the emigrants, to learn from him what was to occur next.

The station platform was teeming with people moving in haphazard directions. Off to his right stood a collection of passengers, pressing inwards to hear someone speaking. Centered in this hive of activity was the agent, waving his arms with expressive animations, speaking at once in several languages, Ukrainian among them. He was announcing that the great ship, the Franz Joseph, would be docking in Trieste in five days.

Passengers reacted with hostility. Some spat on the platform, others shouted at him, or mumbled obscenities that were heard only by those near them.

They were all tired and restless, and Nicholas was that, and hungry too. He had not eaten adequately since he left home, not because it was unavailable, but because it was expensive. His financial resources were minimal, and he was far from lush Manitoba, where he felt assured good food would sustain him. But there was no choice; he would have to make the best of it. He had rushed to pack, ridden a rough wagon all night to Chernovtsi, rushed to get on the train, and was crowded into wooden seats with no room to stretch out to sleep. Rush, rush, rush — only to arrive and have to wait for five days. There was reason to be upset; the agent got an earful from many of the more mature men, and some hostile remarks from women too.

The accommodation that was provided was a matter even more demoralizing. It was a warehouse near the docks, with a rough plank floor, and infested with creatures from the sea, the likes of which Nicholas had not seen before. It was on this floor that he and the others had to wait out the next five days. There were no cots or beds; each had to sleep on the belongings they had with them. In Nicholas's case, it was his white cloth bag in which he carried his clothes, a few articles of personal interest to him, and a few that were deemed important for survival in Canada. Among these was a cherished stone from the bank of the Dniester River, discovered by his father, who then had spent many hours shaping it as a sharpening stone: a gift to his son.

A large kitchen was set up along part of one wall of the warehouse. The idea of food was profoundly inviting, but the odor was strange. Nicholas had never eaten food with that odor, but his hunger was dominant; he overcame his reluctance and handed his bowl to the server to fill. Handed back to him was goulash, a potato soup with substantial pieces of very dark meat floating in a greasy broth. He sniffed the first spoonful. The smell was strange and unappealing, but his stomach was craving sustenance. Holding his breath, and squinting his eyes,

Nicholas chanced eating it. The taste was odd, but much better than he had anticipated.

Later, Nicholas discussed the odd meat in the stew with his friends. They winked at each other, and emphatically announced that it was horsemeat. They had eaten much of it in the military. The extreme dark color confused them a bit, they said, but they assured Nicholas that the horse had died from a natural cause, probably old age. That judgment did not add at all to its appeal, yet it was to be the main fare during the waiting period.

Time crept by. Impatient to get on board ship and begin his voyage to Canada, Nicholas had to tolerate time's measured pace. He slept on the plank floor with hundreds of others: men that snored, infants that cried as their mothers shuffled to corners for privacy where they could bare their breasts and feed them. It resembled a refugee camp; in fact, it might have been correctly labeled as one. Sanitation was impossible; lice and other insects were multiplying and adding to the occupants' distress.

The one positive note was that the beautiful warm water of the Adriatic was but a short distance from the warehouse. The beach was inundated with immigrants walking into the water, some fully clothed, ridding themselves of the pests, and washing their bodies as best they could. Nicholas was among them.

Before going to the beach, he searched through his carrying bag. In it he found what he knew his mother had included: a square of brown soap, homemade, from a combination of animal fat, lye, oils, and water. There was a cove, invisible from the dock, where men alone bathed, near nude, and he joined them. The soap was highly alkaline and stung as he rubbed it on his skin, but it was a fine cleanser and rid him of the persistent gnawing insects that found refuge in his clothes, armpits, and groin. It was his first full body scrub that he'd had in over a week, and the sensation of cleanliness was overpowering. From then on, Nicholas would visit this cove in the shoreline daily.

# CHAPTER 7

The Franz Joseph, the pride of Austria, the majestic transport vessel, steamed into port with bells ringing and its whistles blowing. Sailors cast huge ropes from her to the dockhands who expertly fastened them to iron tie-downs, instantly immobilizing the great ship. Her motors idled and then stopped. Staircases were locked to the dock and to the ship, and a procession of passengers began to descend.

Nicholas stood back against a railing on the dock. This was a sight of which he had never dreamed. The size of the Franz Joseph was awe-inspiring; he estimated it alone could hold all the inhabitants of Onut together with some neighboring villages.

The first class passengers were allowed to disembark ahead of the others. The men were dressed in suits, stiff collared and cuffed white shirts, and colorful ties bound to their shirts with some brilliant clasp of a kind Nicholas had not seen before. Each man wore a hat and spats, the style of the wealthy at that time. *They must be successful businessmen from Canada*, he thought, *coming to Trieste or other parts of Austro-Hungary to do business, and bring more riches to Canada.*

But the women — Nicholas had never imagined such stunning apparel. Corseted to accentuate the female form, they wore flowing pastel dresses, wide brimmed hats, and buckled high-heeled shoes, so unstable that they depended on support from their menfolk as they descended the gangway. Nicholas's eyes riveted on them; he could scarcely comprehend such elegance. The contrast between his rumpled peasant attire and that of the wealthy Canadians was stark and embarrassing. *How*, he pondered, *could this ship convert to bring me and the rest of these motley immigrants westward having just brought such culture and opulence eastward?*

Stevedores were unloading endless numbers of trunks and suitcases, but not a single piece of luggage that Nicholas could see, resembled his humble carrying bag. *One day*, he thought, *I will own a suitcase like those, and when I travel, I will dress in a suit and wear a hat. I will be seen and admired, just as those men are.*

He had learned from his reading that all non-native Canadians had once been poor immigrants, and their toil and shrewdness made it possible for them to reach the ranks of the elite. He understood the country was rich in wood and in furs; the soil was fertile, and agriculture could be the major industry with which he would be involved.

The next day he heard calls from his agent, marshaling the travelers to follow him to the exiting site, prior to boarding. Nicholas's steps were energetic and his anticipation heightened by all he had witnessed.

The building chosen for this purpose was one similar to the warehouse they had slept in for the past six nights: long and narrow, with a row of tables toward one end where several officials stood. Passengers were required to stand in line, holding their travel documents to have them checked by the officials. Then they would be allowed to pass to a similar building to wait until boarding was permitted. As Nicholas approached the officials, he could see that there was an area behind their tables with a number of chairs. There sat a few clearly dejected men speaking with animation to each other displaying anxiety and anger. Nicholas could not hear what they were saying, but their actions spoke for them. Obviously, they were not permitted to board the ship they had waited for. Whatever their problem, it seemed to Nicholas that they were powerless to change it.

The line moved forward. Nicholas heard the Canadian official barking out a command, "Passport!" Nicholas instantly felt a sick feeling spread over his entire body. His knees shook, his heart raced, and his throat choked.

*My God… my God*! The word *Passport* thrashed through his head, *I don't have a passport*!

His agent had told him one was not necessary. He wasn't crossing any borders from Chernovtsi to Trieste, and Canada did not require a passport.

He glanced around for his agent — he was no longer in the building!

Ahead of him, his companions offered their passports; they were stamped, and the men moved forward with the line.

The official sternly demanded Nicholas produce his passport. He could only open his empty hands, as tears welled up in his eyes. Without a word of explanation, or any sign of sympathy, the official, assertively, waved at Nicholas to follow him to the chairs, where he had seen the dejected men arguing.

Nicholas was devastated. *What on earth should I do?* he asked himself. *Maybe I should leave here and find the agent.* But the other men were not leaving. He chose to wait. Beads of sweat formed on his neck and face, and his heart pounded so forcefully that he could see each pulsation through his garments.

Nicholas could not clear his mind of the agent's advice regarding the need for a passport. He had two weeks before he was to leave Onut, and that should have been sufficient time to obtain one. He had passed the medical exam, had his ticket paid for through his father's labors, had overcome his mother's tears, and now his hopes and dreams to come to Canada — dashed.

A peasant boy, scarcely seventeen years old, totally inexperienced and backward in social status, was now separated forever from his friends from neighboring Chornyi Potik. These friends, who had looked after him, and guided him over the past week, were scheduled to board the Franz Joseph, leaving him, alone, to deal with his crisis.

The remaining ten or so aspirants detained with him were Rumanian, and at least one spoke Croatian, languages he recognized but could not understand. Hours dragged on, darkness descended, powerful whistles blew, and the huge vessel was freed from the dock anchors. Nicholas could see her slowly drifting from the shore and into the open Adriatic. He had missed his ship to Canada.

Only then did the officials return, and in Rumanian and Ukrainian, told the few seated that they needed passports, and that they were to go home. The Rumanians argued and seemed prepared to fight, but it was too late. The ship had sailed, and they had no option but to return to their villages.

Nicholas was desperate. He had to find his agent. Going back to Onut was out of the question. He didn't have enough Austrian money to pay the train fare back to Chernovtsi, let alone begin the process of obtaining a passport and returning to Trieste. And he worried about the ship fare — so expensive — would it be valid later on a different ship? In desperation he searched the area, his mouth dry from tension, his eyes filling over and over with tears that he wiped on his sleeve. His sack felt heavy and wouldn't stay on his shoulder, but kept slipping off as he walked or ran in random directions, searching for the agent that had so wrongly advised him.

Nicholas's thoughts began to take on a more ominous form: *was this whole affair a swindle? Did the agent somehow capitalize on my naiveté?* He sickened at his thoughts: the countless hours of labor that his father must have performed to save enough money to bring him to Canada, the sorrow he had caused his mother, his own disillusionment, and his future ruined. He whispered to himself, *How could I have been so trusting?*

Nicholas felt faint; he needed to stop his search to regain a little strength. He reasoned that he held the ticket in his hand, and of the hundreds that boarded successfully, only he and a few others were excluded. Surely, if the agent were a swindler, he would have swindled many more. A wave of confidence returned. He pressed the ticket to the side of his leg and then carefully inserted it into a safe pocket in his coat.

Nicholas spotted him! The agent was in a heated discussion with some of the Rumanians that were without passports. Nicholas ran to the circle and as soon as there was a lull in the verbal exchanges, he addressed the agent in Ukrainian. His voice was thin, his lips quivered; he could hardly articulate the words of despair that were on his mind. Thoughtlessly, the agent laughed at this sorry boy in total distress. But he quickly ceased his imprudent response, and told Nicholas that the immigration rules had just changed within the past week, and passports were now essential.

But, he said, he would buy Nicholas a train fare back to Chernovtsi, and return to Trieste, as a show of good faith. He had offered the same to the Rumanians. Or, there was a second option. Nicholas could wait in Trieste for two weeks when another ship, the Sophia Hohenberg, would take him to North America. He assured Nicholas that he would personally see to it that he had a passport to take him through the immigration line.

Nicholas thought for a moment: nearly a week to get home, nearly a week to return. He decided it was impractical. He chose to stay in Trieste.

Nicholas's heart weighed heavily. The ship was gone, invisible into the night, and it took with it his hopes and aspirations to get to Canada, meet with his father, and begin building his life. Tears kept streaming down his face, his sleeve now damp from the constant wipes. But he was angry too. The agent, whom he had trusted, had laughed at him when he was so distraught. He cursed him silently, then again, and again, with whispers articulating the words.

He thought he should write to his mother and explain the problem, but he knew she would insist that he return home. That meant leaving again, and suffering for her and for him. No, he would not write. He would bear this out, but the agent had better have a passport for him in two weeks!

He returned to the sleeping quarters, now empty except for one man with a kerchief over his face spraying a pungent chemical onto the floors and walls. It was some sort of toxin, to rid the room of lice and fleas, and whatever other parasitic pests had found a ready source of nutrient from the hundred, or more, sleeping there for the past week.

He left the room and sat on a bench outside the door, and there he came to terms with his situation. He could not survive for two weeks with no extra income and still manage the costs to get to Manitoba to his uncle's home. He had to find work that would keep his financial situation stable. Feeling in charge of his destiny, the next morning he threw his sack over his shoulder and walked to the first residential part of the city, nearest the dock.

# CHAPTER 8

The return of his sense of purpose was invaluable, and Nicholas boldly approached the first house to inquire about work. He rapped on the door; a woman appeared and greeted him in German, watching carefully to see if her language was being understood. Low German was required through his school years as a second language, and he was quite capable in both its understanding and speech.

*"Tante eck not orbeit seeken den teet wart ech no ein Schäp iuah Canada"* he said. (Madame, I need to find work while I wait for a ship to Canada. She looked deeply into his gleaming blue eyes and his handsome young face, and sensed the sincerity of his need. Like so many good-natured German women, she consented to hire him to split the pile of wood in her yard. For this she would feed him, and even pay a little more if he stacked the split wood as well.

Mrs. Müller was kind and generous, and fed Nicholas the same food they ate at their table. The days of horsemeat were over, he thought, along with the odd smelling broth, which even after several days, he

43

had found hard to tolerate. The axe she gave him to use was made of fine steel, and when he honed it sharp with his treasured Dniester stone, the wood split cleanly. He stacked the pile according to the directions from Herr Müller, and a mutual respect began to grow.

For his board and the stipend, Nicholas worked diligently during the day and returned to the warehouse at night to sleep. Eventually, Müller's maid took his extra clothing and washed and ironed it, and he did not have to pay. His behavior was exemplary, and his work ethic appealed to the German family. In a week, he had split and stacked all the wood, and the appreciative Germans found other minor jobs for him to do to keep him occupied and fed. His German language skills slowly improved; communication was less halting, and Nicholas was converting to High German from his basic Low German.

Sunday was a day of rest. Nicholas was not permitted to work, but he was asked to join the family in a church service. He was Greek Orthodox; this family was Lutheran. He had read about Martin Luther in school, but had no idea that there was a faith associated with the man. Early Sunday morning, Nicholas made a trip to the cove where he regularly bathed. The morning air was cool, and the salt water was green and refreshing. He did not stay long; he was anxious to dress in his best. Going to church had always been the most exciting day of the week.

In Onut, his church was built from rough rock, held together with mortar that was always cracking and falling away. The parishioners were constantly repairing the walls of the aged building. From the outside, it resembled a multifaceted structure. Colors of new, old, and ancient mortar seemingly without pattern or reason, distinguished it from the whitewashed surrounding buildings. But its pear-shaped dome was its extraordinary feature. It towered above any other building in the village, and by its structural dominance, it called all believers to worship.

His church was built in the middle of a cemetery, implying that the souls of the dead were a part of every Sunday service. Custom held that following the service, the congregation would visit the graves, control the weeds, and polish the headstones. It was the only church Nicholas knew; it was where he had been baptized and where he had faithfully attended every Sunday, without any memory of an exception. The liturgy was in Greek, and his introduction to the study of Greek in school was directed toward understanding it.

Dressed in the new apparel that he had purchased before he left home, his white shirt starched and pressed by the maid in the Müller household, a bow tie that always seemed to sit askew, Nicholas did look dashing. He arrived at the Müller's, was welcomed, and immediately invited to the table to partake in a breakfast with them.

Müller's daughter had arrived the night before, from somewhere in Trieste, where she was attending a boarding school. She was perhaps a year or two older than Nicholas, with strong features, an angular face, and dark brown curly hair held in place by a clasp at the nape of her neck. In everyday clothing she might not have looked so attractive, but this morning, in her church attire, corseted and with flared crinolines, she resembled the most elegent of the women exiting the Franz Joseph a few days earlier. In Nicholas's eyes, she was beautiful. When Nicholas was introduced to her, she approached him, then stepped back a step and curtsied with grace. He had no idea how to respond to this formality, so he stood erect and simply nodded. Little did he know that this response was precisely the correct one, and it made a strong impression on his hosts, and their daughter, Inga.

A horse drawn carriage arrived shortly after, and the seating arrangement was such that Inga and Nicholas sat next to each other. On the way, she asked about his plans in Canada, and confessed that she too had secret wishes to someday travel there. Nicholas explained to her the opportunities in farming, from land offered free for dedicated men to develop by their own initiative. As best he could, in halting German, he expressed his hopes and aspirations. She listened intently, her dark eyes darting from his lips to his eyes to improve her understanding. Oh, how he wished she could speak Ukrainian, the language through which he could have so vividly described his overwhelming vision of his future life. Inga smiled and nodded, suggesting some understanding of his German, and for the first time that Nicholas could remember, he felt a twinge of need for a woman in his personal life.

The carriage stopped, and the family stepped from it to face a stunning stone structure with huge oak doors, and gothic leaded windows of colorful stained glass, intricately assembled to depict themes of Christ on Earth. Nicholas had never seen such a spectacular building. But instead of a cupola to call him to worship, the building had a tall spire that seemed to pierce into the heavens. The marble stairs were worn from generations of worshipers entering and leaving the building, but the wear did not detract from its architecture. Nicholas was anxious to enter and see how ornate the inside would be.

Many worshipers greeted them as they ascended the stairs to the entrance doors. The Müllers were clearly well known and respected. In each instance they did not fail to introduce their guest, and in each instance, the ladies would mimic precisely Inga's introduction to Nicholas: a step or two forward, one step back and a graceful curtsy. He nodded and smiled, more comfortably from introduction to introduction, since he saw Herr Müller nod precisely the same way he had when he was introduced.

The morning sun was shining through the ornate colors of the stained glass. The rays spread over the pews and across the western wall leaving a rainbow of color shimmering with its reflections on the polished woodwork. It was beautiful — but where were the religious icons? One symbol was present and overwhelming: the cross, a simple tall wooden cross, without the embellished knobs of orthodoxy, without the angled lower foot cross, or the little head cross at the top, and without a single visible inscription carved into it to remind the worshiper of the significance of Christ's sacrifice.

And there were pews to sit on: oak benches stained a rich brown. In Onut, everyone stood, for three hours, a discipline that from youth was demanded and enforced. Here the congregation sat, in relative comfort.

An organ played in the background, a musical instrument and a music form Nicholas had not heard before. It was the major key; only rarely had he heard music in that form. Most of the music he played or whistled was in a melodic minor key. To Nicholas, the organ sounded like a countless number of melodies played together, each independent, yet blended into a perfectly harmonized whole.

The Pastor entered, clean-shaven rather than bearded, wearing vestments similar to an Orthodox priest. He spoke endearingly to the congregation in German — not in Greek. Nicholas was able to understand most of what he said, the first time ever that he was able to grasp the meaning of the welcome. Lutherans seemed to celebrate Christ's life, rather than the solemn depiction of his death that the Orthodox portrayed.

It was different, but still it somehow seemed meaningless. The icons…where were the icons? Without them, there was no depth despite the words that were understandable. When the service ended, a relaxed and congenial atmosphere followed.

As they stepped outside, a distant piercing whistle interrupted their conversation: The Sophia Hohenberg had arrived at the dock! Having almost settled into a comfort zone with Inga and her family, Nicholas was jolted back to the reality that here was his passage into his future. He quickly bid farewell to his new family. Herr Müller reached into his pocket, brought out a substantial roll of bills, and handed Nicholas what amounted to several dollars, more than enough compensation for the work that he had done.

He didn't wait for the carriage to take him back. He walked in the direction of the sound of the ship, returning briefly to the Müller residence to gather his belongings, and then followed the streets southward to the shores of the Adriatic. He would never see the Müllers again, and only later did he come to fully appreciate the valuable assistance they had given him. He didn't write because he had not written down an address, but the thoughts of them and the twinge he felt for Inga lived with him for years.

By the time he reached the shore, the passengers had debarked and the few that remained seemed to be waiting for friends or relatives to arrive. Those he saw contrasted with the passengers on the Franz Joseph. They were dressed well but not with the striking attire that he had seen on the First Class Passengers a few weeks earlier. He was still in his Sunday best and felt totally comfortable in their midst. The experiences in Trieste were not a loss; they left life-long impressions, helped build his character, and he would reflect on them for years to come.

It would be another five days that the comparatively uninspiring Sophia Hohenberg would require before she was readied to sail. Clanging of mauls against steel came from somewhere below decks, as workmen seemed to be trying to straighten the hull or repair the engines. Meanwhile, crates of foodstuffs were rolled into her holds by dockworkers. She was not old, it was obvious, but the black paint on her hull peeled in places exposing the underlying metal to rust.

Large though she was, she was significantly shorter than the Franz Joseph. She had three large smoke stacks, each supposedly serving an engine below. The truth? There were only two engines. The third stack was used as an advertising gimmick in order to place her in a category of great ocean liners.

Nicholas paid little attention to the ship's physical state. He was anxious for her to be made ready for the trip to the other side of the world. Now rejuvenated from his depressed state two weeks earlier, he made regular trips to the dock to follow the progress of her preparation.

Immigrants and travelers to America were gathering on the dock. Most seemed to be speaking languages foreign to Nicholas, but three men were talking in a cadence that resembled Ukrainian. Nicholas edged closer. Yes, indeed it was Ukrainian, and he approached them. They halted their discussion and looked quizzically at this approaching stranger. "Where are you travelling to?" Nicholas asked.

"And what is it to you?" one responded.

Nicholas realized that they were cautious to the point of rudeness, so he changed his approach and introduced himself more effectively. "I have been here for over two weeks because I do not have a passport to Canada. My agent had promised that he would obtain the necessary documents to allow me to board this ship. My father and uncle are already in Canada." One of the men answered, "We have passports and we are also going to Canada. We are from Chornyi Potik, a little village in Bukovina."

"Chornyi Potik!" Nicholas exclaimed, "I am from Onut, and the two friends that helped me this far were from your village."

He spoke their names. They knew them, and told Nicholas that news had already arrived in the village that they had safely crossed the ocean and were in Montreal, preparing to travel westward to Winnipeg. A pang of envy came over Nicholas; he should have been there too. But this ship was being readied, and he would soon be in Canada. Just the passport was not in his pocket, and that left him with a gnawing feeling.

Nicholas's new acquaintances proved to be congenial people. They were now housed in a smaller warehouse where the food was better than before, although horsemeat was still the likely meat source. The incessant hammering in the ship's belly finally ceased, and the stewards too, appeared to have completed much of their preparatory work for the voyage.

The agent arrived, and Nicholas prayed that he carried the passport with him. As soon as he was able to ask, the agent laughed — again — and said that he was working on it as they spoke. He would borrow a passport from one of the passengers who had already gone through the immigration checkpoint, and Nicholas could use it to gain boarding privileges. Nicholas realized that the agent had done nothing to this point, and that he would have to provide the solution himself. He told him of the men he had met from Chornyi Potik, and that he thought one might be willing to provide a passport in this scheme.

The agent concurred, and he then related his plan to Nicholas. He would arrange the line so that the three gentlemen went through early, and he would then intercept them and bring a passport to Nicholas. Nicholas was to be near the end of the line, that way providing maximum time for this plan to work. The tactic was illegal, but Nicholas was desperate enough to chance it. It was either this, or return to Onut, disgraced and broke.

In the confusion on the dock, and in the housing quarters, Nicholas lost track of his friends, and was unable to relate the plan to them. The boarding time had arrived, and again the agent was busy aligning the passengers for their medical exams, and then forming a second line to pass through the immigration staff. Nicholas passed the medical exam that consisted, as before, of an eye examination. The agent shuffled him toward the end of the line, and he could see his friends from Chornyi Potik well ahead of him. He pointed them out to the agent, who then immediately approached them and began to talk.

Nicholas's heart missed countless beats. The conversation went on for some time; *Obviously*, Nicholas thought, *the friends were not impressed with offering their passports.* They went through immigration with no problems and the agent resumed his conversation with them. Now, Nicholas was beginning to panic. The chairs that were used for the unsuccessful candidates for Canada were supporting several clearly discouraged individuals. His whole body shook from fear.

With only a few more ahead of him approaching the Immigration Staff, the agent returned and without a word, pressed himself against Nicholas and firmly pushed a passport into his hand. A great sense of relief passed over Nicholas, color rushed back into his cheeks, and he approached the immigration officer with confidence.

Passport!" the official demanded, his eyes showing fatigue from a long day at his post.

Nicholas handed him the passport and held the ticket for him to see. He glanced at the medical exam and didn't even open the passport, simply passed it to his assistant who, similarly, didn't take the time to examine the previous stamp, and stamped it again. Nicholas's legs felt as though they were made of rubber, but he quickly shouldered his white bag and exited before someone could become the wiser. He was on his way to Canada!

The stairs to the deck of the ship were long and steep, but to young Nicholas they were no more than a walk in the park. No other passenger sprang up the stairs like he did. His bag over his shoulder seemed weightless, and even the salt air tasted sweet. On deck, waiting for him, was his savior, his friend from Chornyi Potik who had lent him his passport. With a broad smile, Nicholas embraced him and returned his double-stamped document.

A ship employee pointed in the direction they should go. It was downward, flight after flight of stairs until they had reached the near windowless bottom, the least expensive passenger space on the ship. The smell of human sweat mixed with engine room exhaust should have been nauseating, but not to Nicholas; he was on his way to a land of fortune, and this condition was temporary and insignificant.

That evening, the tie downs were released and the great ship floated free from the dock. The engines revved a bit as the Sophia Hohenberg began her journey out of Trieste and into the deep waters of the Adriatic Sea.

Nicholas secured a bunk, steel tubing welded into a cot for one passenger, adjacent to the engine room wall. The bottom bunks were assigned to women and children, the second tiers to their husbands or elderly, and the top tier to single young men or women. It was into this last category that Nicholas was assigned. He threw his sack onto the bunk and lay for just a minute. The excitement was overwhelming; he descended the ladder and made his way back to the stairwells and up to the deck. He looked out and watched the receding shoreline of Austro-Hungary and the faint lights of Trieste.

The date was April 14, 1906, the weather warm and the winds calm. He stayed on deck for a few hours enjoying the site of the wake as the ship plowed its way southward toward the Mediterranean. He finally felt exhaustion overcoming him, and made his way back to his bunk.

A few children were crying; some mothers were sitting up, shying their breasts as they nourished their infants. The snoring of men mingled with the constant thumps of eccentric shafts, and the grinding of engines that turned them. It was not an environment conducive to sleep, but Nicholas was young and had always been a good sleeper. He slept through the night, and woke only when the bells rang for break-fast service.

He took a place in line to use the washrooms. The line seemed as long as he could see, and the older men were suffering from the need to urinate. In time, he reached the toilets; there were no more than six stalls for hundreds of men. His stall had been used several times without flushing, and it had an offensive smell. He flushed it, having learned the mechanism on the train from Chernovtsi, and then flushed it again after he used it. He smiled to himself; at seventeen he considered himself already a seasoned traveler.

*One day*, he thought, I *will admit these experiences to my mother, and she will laugh and hug me as she always does when I make her happy*. Thoughts like this one came to him as he washed his face with water in a steel sink. Those opportunities would never transpire. About this time, someone was writing a letter in Canada to someone in Onut — a letter that would change Nicholas's life forever.

# CHAPTER 9

Sometime later, the ship changed its course to the west as it rounded the boot of Italy. Now in the Mediterranean, it made its way to the open Atlantic, from which it would not be in sight of land until it reached the shores of North America. The weather remained calm and warm with a slight breeze formed by the motion of the vessel.

Nicholas spent hours on deck during the day observing ocean life. Numerous forms rose from the depths, surfacing momentarily only to disappear below the blue-green of the endless water. Sometimes these animals would be so close to the hull of the ship that he could make out their eyes, and he wondered if they were staring, unblinking, at him as he was staring at them.

There were flying fish that he particularly enjoyed. They would leap from the water flapping their wing-like lateral fins, and travel airborne remarkable distances, their long sleek bodies flashing in the sun, and water droplets creating miniature rainbows beneath them. Then their bodies would move into a dive attitude, their fins hesitating, and they would gracefully return to the depths. Such grace, such beauty Nicholas had not seen before, living in land-locked Bukovina. Again, he wished his mother were with him so that they could share the wonders of sea life together.

The Sophia Hohenberg seemed like a machine in perpetual motion. Her motors never changed their timbre, and the thump of a cam never altered its rhythm. Smoke and steam flowed steadily from two smoke stacks, but the third, in the aft of the boat, remained dysfunctional, serving as a constant false reminder to the passengers that should extra power be necessary, it too would join with the others to help heave this mass of steel across the Atlantic.

Nicholas was comfortable. He joined with others on deck in conversations that were sometimes enlightening and at other times inquisitive. For his age, and coming from a tiny peasant community, he was well read. His school had a few books in Ukrainian that he had absorbed, and several more in German that were technical, and more difficult for him to read. Some Ukrainian books were written about orthodoxy, its mysticism, and its supposed power over the human spirit. One book, however, contained the poems of Ukraine's greatest poet, Taras Shevchenko, and this book was his favorite. It was relatively new to his school's book collection — it could hardly be called a library — and in his free moments, he would tiptoe to the front of the room and bring the book back to his seat.

Free reading time was infrequent. The headmaster of the school was responsible for teaching in the tradition of the eastern periphery of the Empire. Besides learning three languages, students were taught a foundation in mathematics and sciences.

Most literature was directed toward an understanding of the events of the Bible, so lessons on poets such as Shevchenko were rare. Only after having completed the assigned lessons did Nicholas have the liberty to delve into such superfluous readings — such was the headmaster's opinion. However, Shevchenko remained imbedded in Nicholas's mind, perhaps even became an integral part of his psyche for the rest of his life. He often quoted brief poetic passages from that book, by a poet who may have been the first open literary revolutionary against Russian Czarism.

Here on the Mediterranean, basking in spring sunshine, hundreds of people leaned against the ship's railing. This, on their first occasion experiencing release from the toil of providing for the day's sustenance, they thanked the Lord for the gift of a better life to come.

Somewhere on the Atlantic, two ships passed each other — the Sophia Hohenberg sailing to America, the other, sailing to Europe. In the cargo of the ship to Europe was a letter addressed to someone in Onut, and it would be delivered in the week before Nicholas reached the shores of America.

In the mid-Atlantic, perhaps in the area of the Bermuda Triangle, a great storm was developing. The sky had become overcast; the winds began to raise the waters into swells. The ship's engines squealed, drastically different from their normal monotonous drone, their pitch varying with each crash of seawater against the ship's hull.

Not a single passenger remained on deck. Sailors scurried from location to location, grasping the railings or the handholds on the walls as they carried out their duties. The passengers were directed to return to their quarters. All were uneasy, some already sick from the tossing and heaving of the Sophia Hohenberg, and the unpleasant smell of fuel and exhaust soon mixed with the stench of vomit.

The violence of the storm increased by the hour until the great ship was pitched upward and downward, side to side, and at times seemed to turn on an axis to face east instead of west.

The motors raced and the cams pounded, producing more fumes, and now fear. Mothers cried as they cuddled their screaming children; hardy men, unable to reach the washroom, vomited in their cots; youngsters lost control of their bladders and bowels, urinating and defecating wherever they were. The stench was overwhelming and the noise deafening.

For two days and three nights the sky vented its wrath upon the ocean and whatever craft dared brave the ocean surface. Little food was served; dehydration was setting in on the passengers in the lower decks. Somewhere on board, Nicholas heard, people had died.

More suddenly than it had begun, it was over. The Sophia Hohenberg had survived a major Atlantic storm, a credit more deserved by the Captain and crew than by the structure of the vessel itself. The third engine never fired up because, it was then learned, there was no third engine installed. One of the two engines that had brought the ship through the storm was damaged and now only provided minimum power. Someone began sledge pounding; was it in a vain effort to restore full power? Another storm could sink the ship... so the gossip ran.

Sailors came and asked everyone who could still walk to make their way to the deck for water, fresh air, and food, if any appetite remained. Some, including Nicholas, were able to climb the stairs, but more than half, particularly women and children, were too weak to make the ascent. The sailors brought water and food to those who could not leave their bunks, to rehydrate and sustain them. With pressure hoses, buckets, and mops, they began the sordid task of swabbing the floor and bunks of vomitus and excrement.

Nicholas's knees were weak from hours of vomiting; his head pounded from pain, and his balance was scarcely enough to support him upright. Despite relatively calm water, he needed both hands to grasp the rail, as every hint of a motion seemed destined to topple him. His youth was an advantage. As the day lingered on, he began to recover his balance and his headache subsided. He was unable to eat, but he was able to drink water to restore his body's need for fluid.

The wake from the ship was visibly diminished as one engine alone was forced to maintain the course. They were now behind schedule, and there was yet half the Atlantic to cross. When he returned to the lower billets that evening, the area smelled of disinfectant, so strong that it obscured the exhaust and the stench that had inundated the entire quarters that morning. The ship's staff had done an exceptional job of cleaning and disinfecting that formidable space, thereby lessening the chance of a breakout of serious illness.

Children still whimpered, but there was conversation, something that had been missing for the last while. Each day the health of the passengers improved, and soon more of them were gathering on the deck. Each day the sailors would repeat disinfecting the quarters.

Twenty days into the voyage someone spotted a thin dark line on the western horizon. It was land! The sailors confirmed that what was visible was the shores of New York, not Halifax or Montreal as Nicholas had anticipated, but New York…in the United States. Nicholas did not know whether the injured Sophia Hohenberg had changed her course for repairs, or whether this was her original destination. He had not given it much thought throughout the days on the ocean. He knew he was going to Canada, and that was all he needed to know. Now he would have to make his way northward, but his resources for the extra travel were limited.

Small watercraft became visible, darting in and out of view on the skyline; seagulls screamed and circled the ship like an honor-guard as the dark line on the horizon became more distinct. On the morning of the twenty-first day after leaving Trieste, the Sophia Hohenberg entered the Hudson Canal. The decks were crowded as the toiling ship passed Liberty Island with its Statue of Liberty, her majestic arm raised in welcome.

Nicholas had read about the statue, a gift from the French to the Americans in respect of their newly gained independence. The reading had excited him, and he had hoped one day he might see her. Now she was but a few hundred yards from the side of the deck he was standing on. It was the warmest of welcomes to the new land, and the sensation ran through his whole body causing a rush of goose pimples to spread from his shoulders to his feet.

He was in America!

Here was freedom and opportunity. Somehow he would get to Canada where there was freedom and opportunity too. His dream was becoming a reality.

Unknown to Nicholas, while in the midst of the great storm, some-one's letter to another in Onut had been delivered. Nicholas would never know who wrote it, even questioned if such a letter had ever been written, but it, supposedly, was from Canada. It was purported to tell the story of Nicholas's illness on board ship, his death, and his burial at sea.

It created an immediate rumor in Onut, and the gossip, that was to be restrained from Elana, his mother, and the children, was hurriedly related to her, as gossipers cannot wait to do. Elana could not believe the words. Her breath froze, she gasped, stumbled onto a stool, all color drained from her face, the room swirled, and her speech numbed. The bearer of the news embellished it with the consequences of omens and superstitions: of burial in a white sheet, perhaps the cloth from the bag Elana had sewn for him; how his naked body sank into the ocean depths, the white sheet floated to the surface, and remained there, as the ship moved from it.

Death was no stranger to the peasantry, but death was dealt with by tradition and custom. Separate from these traditions and customs were omens, often perpetrated by the clergy, who used their station to frighten the submissive populace with auguries that only they alone could dispel. Burial at sea itself brought trepidation, but to be buried in a white sheet, in infinite water, was a vision with which Nicholas's mother could not cope. Her beloved son, her pride, her hopes for him, not only lost through death, but committed to some eternal damnation by being wrapped in a white cloth she may have sewn for him, multiplied to create the most forbidding of all possible outcomes. On the 4rd of May 1906, as Nicholas first marveled at the faint sight of the shores of America, unknown to him, horrified by the news the rumor had brought her, Elana, his mother, died.

# PART II

# CHAPTER 10

American seamen boarded and guided the ailing Sophia Hohenberg into the docks at Ellis Island. Huge ropes were thrown to men on shore who secured the bow and the stern to the dock anchors. Nicholas had already packed his bag with his belongings and stood anxiously in line to leave the ship.

The gangways were lowered, and first and second-class travelers were given first opportunity to disembark. It seemed to be taking forever. Some had to be supported, having still not recovered from seasickness. But eventually, Nicholas's line began to move. Finally he stepped onto the dock, but his sea legs found the shore unstable, and he nearly fell. Others around him grasped at railings to gain support. It was an odd feeling, one that Nicholas would not experience again.

He followed the long line to immigration where he was asked his name, nationality, race, last residence, his destination, and the amount of money in his possession. He pronounced his name as Nickolai Voroniuk, going to Winnipeg, Manitoba, to his uncle Iwan, and he counted out $8.25 remaining in his pocket. The man recorded his name as Nykolaj Woroinuk, and the rest of the information. He now had new names, Nykolaj and Woroinuk, and would keep these for a short while. The official marked him as *alien* since his destination was in Canada and not the United States. No passport was requested, and he was free to find his way to Manitoba.

New York already had a substantial Ukrainian speaking community from the first wave of mass immigration to the United States some 35 years earlier. It was common for these residents to meet the ships coming from Europe carrying Ukrainian-speaking immigrants, in the hopes that news of their loved ones in the old country would drift back to them. One such family noticed Nicholas, clearly disoriented, using Ukrainian to find a way to a train station. They approached him in his own language.

They invited him to stay and rest but he was long overdue from his expected date of arrival and was anxious to get to Stuartburn, Manitoba, where his uncle lived and his father often visited. He wanted to take the earliest train to the border, and then on to Winnipeg, then to Emerson, from where he would walk to Stuartburn. This gracious family added enough money to his resources to make it possible for him to reach his destination and buy food as well.

This was Nicholas's first experience with genuine kindness in a foreign land, and he was impressed. He wrote down their address and promised to refund the money as soon as he was able.

The train took him to Montreal where he should have disembarked weeks earlier from the Franz Joseph. He took the train to Winnipeg and Emerson. Then, his money virtually exhausted, he began his fifty-kilometer walk to Stuartburn.

The walk was across relatively flat country with farms on either side of the road, lush green with the new wheat sprouting in every direc-tion he looked. Little dwellings and small farmsteads appeared near the road each half-mile, rather than the community living that he had left in Austria. It was different, and it was beautiful.

Nicholas was happy to be near his destination, but the walk was long, and he wasn't going to reach Stuartburn even if he walked all night. His options were to knock on a door or make a bed of boughs and sleep outdoors. The success at knocking on a door in Trieste prompted him to choose that approach. As he walked up the roadway to the next farmhouse, a large brown dog barked, its tail wagging excitedly in greeting. It was dusk, the door opened long before he reached it, and a short robust woman with her two children walked forward to meet him.

"*Guten Abend,*" she greeted.

"*Guten Abend, meine Dame,*" he cheerfully replied. Germans again. He had such good luck with them before; maybe it would hold in Canada.

Nicholas explained that he was from Austria, his German not so good, and he was walking to Stuartburn. He was tired, and would like shelter to spend the night.

"Ja, gut. Aber Sie müssen hungrig sein?" she asked. (Yes, good, but you must be hungry?)

"*Ja,, ich bin hungrig, oba ech well die nich baudern aus blos fan eh staed tom schlopen.*" he stated, reverting back to his low German (Yes I am hungry but I don't want to burden you except for a place to sleep).

The children leaped with joy and raced to the house to open the door for Nicholas. Overwhelmed by the kindness this gracious woman displayed, he again committed himself to one day show the same warmth and concern for other people in need. He could not have known that one day he and his wife would be recognized and admired for their generosity.

Her husband came from outside and she introduced him to Nicholas. He was a husky man with gnarled hands and a lined face, and he too was kind, like his wife. The children romped around the room, wrestling each other one moment and chasing each other the next, trying to attract Nicholas's attention. Visitors were infrequent, and Nicholas's presence was an opportunity for all of them to enjoy his company.

These Germans had immigrated to Canada some ten years earlier. At that time, they were as destitute as Nicholas, and were treated well by Irish settlers who came before them. In the ten years, they had managed to build a log house, own animals, and sow a quarter section of fine land to wheat that looked as though it would produce a substantial crop that year. Canada, they said, is even better than the advertisements that induced them to move here in the first place.

The table was set for Nicholas alone; they had eaten earlier. The children sat on either side of Nicholas and watched every move he made. A large plate of sauerkraut with pork meat was placed before him. Another dish was heaped with potatoes, and coffee was brewing on the cabin stove. This would be the best meal he had eaten since leaving the Müllers in Trieste.

In Onut, food was served in a large bowl placed in the center of the table and dinner guests reached in and spooned out as much as they wanted. For soup and other liquids, a dipper was used. There were dishes, knives, and spoons, but no forks. The first fork that Nicholas had seen and learned to use was on the train to Trieste. A fork was placed before him now, and when prompted to eat, he carefully stabbed the meat and the sauerkraut and moved it to his plate. He felt civilized by the skill with which he was able to manage this task, and he secretly smiled to himself. But no one paid attention except the children; the parents were deeply engrossed in the story he related in imperfect German.

They told Nicholas their children would not be able to go to school because the distance to a school was too great. Maybe one day they would be able to go and learn English, but until then, they would speak German and the parents would school them in basic mathematics and history. This took Nicholas aback; school had been such an important part of his life.

The children were moved from their sleeping area to the parents' room, and Nicholas was given the children's place for the night. To him, it suggested that generosity surfaced in those that had experienced hardship. He wondered if, with no further hardship, would generosity disappear? He vowed to never allow that to happen to him.

The lessons of life were making an impression. He had doubted his Jewish agent when he didn't have a passport for him. He had almost dismissed him as a fraud when he had returned to Trieste having done nothing about obtaining one. But through the agent's shrewd negotiating, he had made it to Canada, and he realized that this man was at least faithful to his word.

One of the men from Chornyi Potik had allowed his personal passport to be used for Nicholas to pass through immigration, an illegal act that might have cost him his freedom to come to Canada.

There were the Müllers, then the Ukrainian speaking Americans in New York, and now these Germans in Manitoba. Yes that must be it: Generosity is nature's gift to man. Nicholas felt the desire to mimic each of them, and he hoped that life would offer him the chance to do so.

He slept well but not long. Before sunrise he was on the road, the final leg of his journey to Stuartburn. It was May 10, 1906; it had taken over two months from the date he left his home in Onut to arrive at his destination in Manitoba.

By mid-afternoon he saw Stuartburn rising in the distance. Someone who knew Uncle John well gave him directions to his homestead.

John's wife, his Aunt Sanchira, was working in the garden when Nicholas called to her. She recognized him instantly, dropped her hoe, and rushed to greet him. The embrace from a woman so like his mother was warm and comforting. It instantly brought memories of his last moments with her at the gate in Onut. Tears flowed. Time had passed since he left home, and only now did he realize how much he had missed the feel of a woman's hair against his face, the softness of her back in his hands and her breasts pushed against his chest. They parted, but holding hands, looked at each other with tears streaming down their faces, then hugged again.

Sanchira called to the house, "Peter, Eliza, come out. Your cousin Nicholai has arrived from Onut!"

In a moment, the door flew open and out bounded Elizabeth followed by the slow moving Peter. Elizabeth, fourteen years old, rushed to Nicholas — but she stopped a few paces short. She was nearly as tall as he and had begun to develop the features of a woman, and with them came a degree of self-consciousness. Meeting a boy almost her age, rushing toward him clearly intent on embracing him, was suddenly embarrassing. She stood motionless, as blood rushed to her neck and face making her fully aware that she was blushing intensely.

Nicholas noticed, and eased the moment by saying, "Elizabeth, my goodness, you have grown so much since I last saw you. You are a beautiful young woman and I am so glad to see you again." Elizabeth did not move, however, still shocked by her forwardness. Nicholas moved a step or two forward, stopped, looked at her slender body from head to foot, took another step forward, and gently embraced her. Elizabeth stood stalk still, seemingly paralyzed, unable to respond either in action or in word.

By now Peter had made his way to the group. He was ten, and wore a broad smile of sincere welcome for a cousin he could not remember. He had been just a child when the family chose to immigrate to Canada, arriving with one of the earlier waves of Ukrainian speaking Austrians. He grasped Nicholas's coat, and Nicholas pressed Peter's head to his waist. Ah, family again. What a long time it had seemed. But he was now home, a new home, in a strange but beautiful country.

Later, his uncle John came from working on the land. It was another exciting reunion, and the whole family spoke of the tribulations they had experienced before finally reaching Stuartburn. John and Sanchira's oldest daughter, Domka, had already left home, married, and was living some distance away.

They talked late into the evening, and Nicholas was able to relate marriages, births, and deaths in Onut that were of intense interest to the isolated John Woroniuk family. They, in turn, told about their difficult times over the past years, but how things were getting better. There was food, and the farm was becoming profitable. John said he would take Nicholas around the property in the morning. By Onut standards, John was already a successful farmer.

Aunt Sanchira served dinner; daylight turned to darkness, two candles were lit and the family discussion began to dwindle and the eyes of the children fluttered and closed. Little Peter fell asleep, his head turned to one side on the table and one hand hanging down between his knees. They prepared a bed for Nicholas in the corner of the room — of willow boughs bent into a cradle form with moss and reeds substituting for a mattress. But he slept well and did not rise until Sanchira was stoking the stove for breakfast.

They ate a simple meal of porridge from cornmeal and milk, and then Nicholas accompanied his uncle outdoors to look at what he had achieved in a few years in Canada.

His homestead was a full 160 acres, more land than many estates in Bukovina. He was clearing the land year by year and sowing it to wheat and oats. There was a cow that provided milk for the family along with butter and cheese, a team of workhorses, a plow, and a set of harrows. The equipment was old and worn. John had been able to barter his labors with wealthy local farmers for used equipment to begin his farming operation. By modern standards, this operation was doomed to failure, but in 1906, it had potential for success. It would need only time, and the provision of heavy labor.

Nicholas could see this even at his age, and he inquired whether homestead land was available somewhere near Stuartburn. John advised him that Austro-Ukrainians and German Mennonites had taken up all the good land. He said the nearest homestead land available was to the east where Nicholas's sisters and husbands had settled. That land was rocky, and they were having a difficult time growing anything other than hay.

The next day, Nicholas packed his belongings and set out to find his father, then working on the railroad in Minnesota on what was called an *extra gang*. Extra gangs were men hired, under the supervision of an experienced railroad man, to move from location to location, maintaining the railbed, replacing old ties or bent rails, and living in makeshift bunks for a day or two before moving again.

While aboard the Sophia Hohenberg, and during his first days in Canada, Nicholas had learned a few English words, and these he practiced as he walked to the international border. At the railroad office, he was able to ask for his father by name. He learned that George had left his job to take up work clearing land for a wealthy farmer nearby.

Nicholas entered the farmer's property and asked about the location of his father, and they told him how to find him in the woods. Nicholas saw him from a distance, and his heart raced as he approached him. Finally he called out, now just a few steps away, "Father, it is Nicholai."

George Woroniuk had been expecting his son for the past few weeks and had become worried that his trip over such a long distance had not gone well. Hearing his voice was a joyous moment that he would recall all his life. "Nicholai," he shouted, "God has guided you to me! At last, at last, I have you with me!"

He had his son with him, two daughters not far away, and the rest of the family would soon be reunited. Like Nicholas, he had no idea that his wife was no longer alive.

George was impressed with Nicholas's physical stature, and as he continued to work, he taught. He showed Nicholas the skill of cutting down trees and gave him his axe to practice his skills right there and then. The first several trees were troublesome. The glance of the axe from the downward cut would sometimes spring away, and the blade would careen from the tree narrowly missing Nicholas's leg. But he soon learned to angle the blade correctly, and the tree would eventually fall. He was far from an expert woodsman, but he had learned the fundamentals. Practice would perfect his skills. Every few trees, George would sharpen his axe with a stone similar to Nicholas's, also retrieved years before from the banks of the Dniester.

Nicholas's upper body was not strong; he had not worked to harden it for the life as a tree faller. He had helped with harvest in Onut, was competent with the sickle and scythe, could tie bundles from the cut grain, and had thrashed it with long flails. He had the body form, but it was not yet honed for cutting trees.

The farmer hired Nicholas to accompany his father in clearing his land of oak. He was paid $1.50 for 10 hours of work and he worked with his father at this job for over four months. He was deducted 60 cents per day for food and another $1.00 per month for medical. His savings amounted to $19.00 per month. His father gave him money to buy a good axe. It served him so well that it became a memorable possession. He cherished it for the rest of his life.

From the other workers who spoke English, Nicholas learned new words. His vocabulary was growing rapidly, but sentence structure remained a mystery. As a tree faller, his skill was soon recognized. His short stature made it convenient for him to cut the tree several inches closer to the ground and he did not have to limb the tree so high, as did taller men, to access the trunk. Once his hands calloused, and his muscles adapted to the labor, he became one of the best fallers in the group.

When winter approached, the farmer no longer needed help. The snow would soon come, trees would be buried in it, and time would be wasted clearing a field of snow around trees prior to cutting. "Inefficient use of labor," the shrewd farmer said. Paying for inefficiency was not to the farmer's advantage. Nicholas learned his first lesson about the balance between labor and its return. The farmer let his workers go to seek other employment.

Nicholas was without work for a few days while he walked to a site in Manitoba, some seventeen kilometers from his uncle's farm, to begin work for the Kruckson Lumber Co., again as a tree faller and trimmer. The wage was about the same, $1.50 per day, or he could work at cutting down a tree for two cents and trimming the useable portion of it for another three cents. The trees were mostly poplar, seldom exceeding eight inches in diameter, and with thinner trunks they were easier to fall. He decided he could do better cutting and trimming for five cents per tree.

On his first day, he met an English-speaking tree faller with whom he would work for two months, a fine, tall young man by the name of

Stanley. Stanley would teach Nicholas English while Nicholas honed his axe with his expert skills using his Dniester stone.

The weather was cold and snow was blowing, a warning of a typical Manitoba winter. Stanley finally persuaded Nicholas to stay at the mill bunkhouse rather than walk to his uncle's in progressively deteriorating weather. The bunkhouse was but a kilometer from the cut site, and the food they served was better than the fare he was receiving at his uncle's home. But he would miss the evening review with Uncle John and the occasional periods when the children were up to worship his presence.

His English was improving by the day. Stanley was an avid teacher, insisting on reasonable pronunciation and grammar. Nicholas was adding a fourth language to his Ukrainian, German and Greek.

Then it happened.

# CHAPTER 11

A letter came addressed to Nicholas from his father and uncle, and delivered to him at the cut site by a youthful employee of the company. Nicholas was excited; perhaps it meant that the rest of the family was coming. He would get to see his mother after nearly seven months, and the sisters that he had teased to distraction before he left Onut. As he opened the letter he was thinking that he would apologize to his siblings. He was a man now; he was earning a living and doing more than an ordinary one-man's job.

He buried his axe into a stump, sat on another, and began to read. He lost his breath immediately, as tears streamed down his face; reading the rest was done in short surges between welling eyes. Stanley noticed and immediately came over.

"What is it, Nicholas?" he asked.

But Nicholas could not answer. His voice had totally ceased to function, and his breathing was in short inhalations between sobs. Finally, with Stanley's hand on his shoulder, he was able to gasp two words:

"Mother dead."

After a few moments of silence, Stanley knelt down in front of Nicholas and said in a most consoling way, "I am sorry, and I know how you feel. My mother is dead too."

"Letter says need to go to father and uncle," Nicholas blurted out. With that he rose to his feet and began to collect his belongings, haphazardly, leaning from time to time against a tree for support.

He removed his axe and began to turn. Then he remembered; he needed to say good-bye to his good friend, so he turned back, re-struck the axe, and began to extend his hand to Stanley. They clasped for a moment and then, anticipating each other's emotions, they embraced. Two hardened men in a forest, standing there in each other's arms, with tears flowing down their faces, both responding to a man's grief. Nicholas tried to tell Stanley that they would meet again, but the words did not come. Stanley understood and nodded as Nicholas turned to walk to camp.

He quit his job, picked up his pay and his bag, and took the trail to his uncle's home. No one knew, at this time, that Elana had prophesied her own fate, except Nicholas. He would not learn the details of her death until he read the letter from his siblings.

Nicholas would never see Stanley again. Somehow, over the two months they had worked together, his last name was never mentioned. Nor did he, in Nicholas's time of grief, ever say from what his mother had died. Stanley, his first Canadian friend, remained in memory throughout Nicholas's life — an experience of changing from a stranger to a friend through the medium of compassion and words.

It was dark when he arrived at his uncle's cabin. The faint light from a wick burning in wax was scarcely enough to identify the two men and one woman sitting at the table. Sanchira held out her arms to him as he entered, stomping his feet to rid them of snow. She was in tears as she hugged him, and then led him to the stove to get warm.

The two men seemed stoic; they nodded to him but did not leave their seats. Nicholas briefly stood beside the stove and then proceeded to the table to join them.

Nicholas's eyes became accustomed to the faint light in the room, and he could see how his father had aged from the news he had received. His strong, straight back was bent, his usually cheerful face segmented with creases that had never before been visible. He was not crying, but it was obvious that he had been. It was months since his wife had died, and now the news finally came to him. George Woroniuk realized how distant Canada was from Bukovina, and what a major impact his absence had made on his family. He handed Nicholas the letter from the children.

It had been written about a month earlier and told of his mother's incredible grief when she received word that Nicholas had died.

The children had tried to live without her, but now it was becoming difficult. Neighbors, who helped originally, were withdrawing and attending to their own needs. Simon, the oldest brother, and his wife, looked after them, but soon had a son of their own, and this too added stress. The children needed their father. They wanted him to come home, as children in need always do. George Woroniuk knew he must return to save the rest of his family.

"Son," he began, "you see from the letter that I have to return to Onut." His voice, hardly audible, "I have saved $80.00, and that is not enough for the passage. Are you able to help, even a little, financially?"

Nicholas had to pause before he was able to speak, his cheeks wet with tears, he answered, "I can, Father, I have saved $123.00 and I can give you all of it, if you need it."

This revelation created a gasp from those around the table. No one expected him to have saved so much in such a brief time.

"You are, indeed, a remarkable man," George said. "Let me have $100.00 and you keep $23.00 for your own needs. I will go back at once and begin arranging to bring your sisters to Canada."

The following morning, the three men departed in a horse drawn sleigh to a railway station where George would begin the trip back to his children whom he had not seen in more than three years.

Nicholas's uncle asked him to stay with them for the winter, help with winter work, and pay only $15.00 for board and lodging for the rest of the season. Nicholas agreed. He needed family to help overcome his anguish. Most troubling to him was that his mother's death could be traced directly to her love for him. His conscience was troubling him; his passion to come to Canada was a factor in her demise.

Nicholas wanted to see his loder sisters, Daria Kostenyk and Elizabeth Kowaliuk, in Arbakka, a day's drive to the southeast. He and Uncle John drove there with the team and sleigh, and the sisters begged him to stay the winter with them. The request provided an opportunity to live with his immediate family, plus they offered to keep him for $10.00 rather the $15.00 that Uncle John was requesting. He chose to make the move.

"Forgive me, Uncle John, I would like to stay with my sisters. They are poor, you can see, and maybe I can help them a little."

John would miss him. Nicholas was a good worker and, in just those few weeks, had materially helped cutting logs to build a new house. Nicholas's skill with his axe was valuable. John did not make a counteroffer to keep Nicholas; he understood the attachment Nicholas had to his immediate family.

Nicholas bought 100 pounds of white flour, 20 pounds of sugar, and a bag of unroasted coffee, for $8.00. The families' immediate appreciation was worth that. However, as the weeks went by, the flour was used, and the coffee roasted and brewed, each cup sweetened with sugar and whitened with cream. Suddenly Nicholas sensed that he had become a burden, and little differences, typical of sibling rivalry, began to creep into their relationships. When April came, Nicholas bid farewell, and left for Winnipeg in search of work.

His first job was in a steel factory where he worked for $1.23 per day and had to provide his own board and room. Staying in a hotel would have left nothing for his savings. Instead, he bunked with other workers and survived on bunkhouse fare. The arrangement had one advantage: it enabled him to continue to improve his English.

When winter came, he returned to the forest where the pay was better and the work much more to his liking. He had saved $200.00, had visited his sisters at Easter, spending a week with them, and then returned to the camp. Before Christmas, Nicholas had saved another $215.00, and the following year, another $300.00.

In the spring of 1910, Nicholas's father, sisters, and son, with his wife and child, arrived in Manitoba. They took homesteads in the Gardenton area, the land equally rocky to Arbakka and unsuitable for grain farming. The family was finally together, except for the loss of Elana, their devoted wife and mother.

By the standards of the time, Nicholas was a rich and eligible young bachelor. Now aged 20, it was time to make an important move. His mind, in his idle moments, returned to Inga in Trieste, to the form of her body, the slight scent from the perfume she used, her eyes, her hair. He realized he needed a woman in his life.

He bought a suit for $15.00, two white shirts, a tie, and a hat. With his new wardrobe, he returned to his sisters in Arbakka, ready to begin courting eligible girls in search of a wife.

Arbakka, like most Ukrainian speaking communities of the early twentieth century, retained many customs from Bukovina. One such custom that favored men was that should any unmarried man ask the father of a single girl for permission to marry her, and the father consented, the deal was struck. The girl, should she refuse, would be committed to spinsterhood; no other man would approach her.

Many single men from Winnipeg would come to farming communities, like Arbakka, to spend the winters where it was less expensive and use this ploy to find a wife. Nicholas knew this custom, and he had already met Erena Lazoruk, an attractive, healthy sixteen year old, a neighbor of his sisters, and he rushed to impress her. He knew that she would be subjected to the city vagabonds in search of available single women, and she could be lost to him. They met at the village dance, and so began a brief but sincere courtship with a woman who was to become his wife.

The Lazoruks were impoverished farmers though they had come to Canada two years before Nicholas. The land they had in Arbakka was not suitable for grain farming. It was wet, low, and rocky, on the western periphery of the Canadian Shield. Eking a living out of this kind of land was impossible.

Erena had two brothers of nearly the same age as Nicholas and he endeared himself to them. They would champion him to the parents when Nicholas would make his critical move.

Nicholas was preparing to approach Erena's father about marriage. Contrastingly, she felt she was too young at sixteen to marry. She had never even considered it. But she knew the custom, and if Nicholas was to propose marriage to her parents, she really had no choice; she would have to say yes.

To say that there was love leading to their marriage would be an exaggeration. However, to say that love would grow out of the marriage is a truth. Nicholas proposed, Yakiew Lazoruk, Erena's father agreed, Erena said "yes," and they were married on November 12, 1911. Erena had turned seventeen ten days before.

It was a typical Ukrainian wedding; festivities lasted for three days. The dowry that Erena presented was a team of remarkable oxen besides the usual quilts and pillows from goose down. Nicholas provided his substantial finances, the envy of the entire community.

When the wedding was over, some guests were suffering from an excess of spirits; others were fatigued from dancing throughout the night to music from a fiddle and a cembalo. Some were lethargic from overeating traditional perogies, cabbage rolls and pork, boiled, fried and salted, and the ubiquitous potato, along with peas, beans, and whatever else guests brought. The bride and groom were more fatigued than the guests; perhaps more inebriated too, since a custom of gifting by each guest was followed with a toast of homemade liquor.

It was a glorious affair, even with the winter winds setting in and a blanket of snow covering the landscape of grass and rock. Nicholas paid the musicians, and they capitalized further by the donation of coins dropped into the "f" holes (artistically carved openings on the top of a violin) as a token for good entertainment. The women, their voices hoarse from singing during the numerous rituals of a Ukrainian wedding, cleared the dishes. They laughed about the ballads they had composed in meticulous rhyme and rhythm, teasing the young couple about their past and future.

As the fiddler was shaking out the coins from inside the body of his violin, Nicholas asked him if he might try to play it for a moment. It had been five years since he had played one, a self-made fiddle in Onut; his futile effort to replace the one his grandfather had destroyed when he was a child. He craved to try this real instrument with real gut and steel strings and a bow with genuine horsetail hair. The fiddler happily offered the violin to Nicholas with a few coins still rattling inside.

Nicholas placed the instrument close to his chin, struck the strings with the bow, and his excellent pitch perception immediately required a more precise tuning. The fiddler was instantly impressed; this young groom had a remarkable ear! He drew the bow to play the first notes of a well-known gypsy theme, and the hair rose on the fiddler's neck and arms. The fingers of his left hand searched for exact positioning, imperfect at first but in repeat attempts, found their spot. The bow, though jerky, was strong and remarkably accurate for his not having held one for years.

This was talent, hidden within the hands and heart, and expressed in the longing tune of the gypsy theme *Doina*. Nicholas apologized for the imperfections, but the fiddler was astounded. Erena, who was helping the women, came to see who had articulated this new tone. She was stunned that it was her husband. She had no idea of his proclivity for music.

To Nicholas, this moment was ethereal. He knew that he must own a violin and play again. Erena tugged at his coat. "Nicholai, Nicholai," she gasped, "I never knew…you never told me…did you know that the violin is my favorite instrument? You have to have one. Right away. Goodness! The tone; I can't believe it!" At that moment he concluded that this woman would stand with him through times good and bad. He was right.

The young couple spent a few days with the Lazoruk family, and the closeness to Erena's brothers matured into a mutually comfortable relationship that would last their lifetimes. Nicholas and Erena Woronuk would not be separated, except through death, for more than forty years.

# CHAPTER 12

Erena had been a mere seven years old when her family immigrated to Canada and immediately settled in Arbakka, directed there by immigration personnel from Winnipeg. The good homestead lands in southern Manitoba were already filed on, and the only land remaining was in the eastern aspect, grassland that appeared largely free of trees and ready for a breaking plow.

But beneath the thin surface of grey topsoil was rock. Rock that regardless how often it was picked, new underlying rock would rise to the surface. Each of the Lazoruk's plots had 160 acres of it, but to the new immigrant, the spread alone seemed to represent an opportunity for the creation of wealth. Their thought was that with repeated picking, the rocks would disappear and great soil would replace it — in reality, after a century of picking, the land is still rocky, camouflaged by a thin layer of sandy soil.

Children were assets. The more children a family had, the more hands there were to pick rocks! Erena was one of four born to Wasylena and Yakiew Lazoruk. As a young girl she was relegated to picking only the smaller rocks, those of a size she could easily lift. Erena joined the family in the field to clear what Yakiew had tilled with oxen and a plow or Wasylena had dug with a spade for a garden. It was wrenching labor, but it may have had one hidden value: it resulted in a powerful physique in a growing child, one that would serve Erena well throughout her long, arduous life.

Arbakka couldn't boast the presence of a school; there were too few settlers there. Besides, there was tradition. In most instances, a girl's gender obviated schooling. It was so in Tovtri, Bukovina, where the Lazoruks emigrated from, and it would be so in Canada. Traditions were hard to break, and even if there had been a school in Arbakka, it is doubtful that girls would have attended.

Their education was to learn to do the traditional chores associated with womanhood: cooking, gardening, cloth weaving, sewing, and always the task of embroidering. But there was more: there was cow milking, cream separating, cheese and butter making, feeding chickens and pigs, hand drawing water from a well or packing it from a stream, heating it, hand washing clothes, drying them in the wind, followed by hours of ironing, and yet find time to entertain the occasional visitor or partake in the village dance. On top of this was bearing and raising children, many children, carding wool, hand spinning it into yarn, plucking the down from ducks and geese, sewing quilts and pillow cases, and finding time to pick rocks, hopefully exposing a little more soil to seed.

The education of girls was directed to mastering the art of survival, not the intellectual stimulation achieved from reading a book. In the immigrant's mind, a woman's education would have cut deeply into her ability to master essential tasks. Thus, a man in search of a wife looked for skills, strengths, and childbearing physical features.

Erena never did see the inside of a classroom. Before she married, she had never read a word nor understood numbers beyond being able to count them. But the skills that were necessary for a good wife to possess, she had mastered. Nicholas, in search of a mate, saw in her a partner in his quest for success: a healthy, erect, gracious young woman who could work all day, from summer's early sunrise to its late sunset, rest a bit, and do it again. He was impressed, not in love, but impressed with this young woman. That was what was necessary when he chose her for his wife.

Nicholas discovered later, that hidden beneath this cloak of traditional womanhood, was a bright and revolutionary spirit. Erena would soon begin discarding superfluous traditions and concentrate those saved hours on providing for a better life. She first ceased embroidering, which took countless hours that could be spent more productively. Later, she would discard other Orthodox traditions that were seen in Canada as characterizing her Eastern European culture as an identifiable minority. Her intelligence and tenacity surfaced constantly, admired by some, shocking to others, but these traits created an enduring bond with her husband.

Erena's two brothers were returning to the jobs they had left in order to attend the wedding, and Nicholas was anxious to return to the forest where his expertise with his axe created income. In a week, he left his new bride and set off for Winnipeg. He travelled to new lumber mills that were springing up to service this rapidly growing city.

Erena, left with her mother and father in Arbakka, dedicated herself to the tasks that would make her a better wife. She learned about childcare from her sister-in-law, Maria Lazoruk, who already had three children of the thirteen she would eventually bear, and who was known in the community as an excellent mother and housewife.

Erena had seen her husband reading a newspaper and longed to make sense of the unique characters that formed the words, which when strung together, created meaning. Nicholas would have to teach her to read. There was no alternative— he would have to do it! "No children of ours will be so limited," she argued. "Schooling for them will be a priority."

On each occasion that Nicholas returned to his wife, he would review with her the letters of the Ukrainian alphabet, and have her memorize the sounds that they represented. Soon Erena was able to combine the letters together, and the magic of words appeared. Simpler and more practical than English, in that respect, reading in Ukrainian was, nevertheless, considered a waste of effort within Arbakka's women's circle.

What was Erena trying to do, become a politician? Not a letter she was rehearsing, nor the words that ensued, would feed a louse let alone her husband! So the gossip provided fodder for the woman-folk, but it was the first of a number of revolutions she would initiate.

Like all female children, she had been taught to embroider the course linen cloth that was woven on looms by the women in her native Tovtri. The cloth was unyielding, and its only attractive feature was the colorful thread and beadwork designs that symbolized each Ukrainian-speaking area. She became skilled in this art form but despised the wasted time it required. The availability of cotton broadcloth in Canada, with its printed patterns, was her salvation. She would not embroider another piece of clothing for the rest of her life.

Through the winter months of 1911-12 she collected essential items for their home-to-be. She obtained a Jersey calf that she would raise and pet to a point where the young animal followed her like a devoted dog. By spring the calf had become a cow, she had calved, and was producing milk. Erena would need this milk, for by that spring she was clearly showing the physical characteristics of pregnancy: she would have a child. Nicholas was working in the woods and making decent wages; life was good. He would soon get a homestead and they would build a house and raise their family.

In September, their firstborn was a son, and they named him George, after Nicholas's father. Nicholas had been home for several days prior, helping with the Lazoruk farm duties, among which rock picking was a major responsibility. The Lazoruks had sown wheat and oats, but the barren sandy soil could only sustain the oats, valuable for feed for the animals but insufficient in yield to constitute a market. Natural grasses grew, but they only made hay. The animals would be well fed, but humans could starve on such land.

# CHAPTER 13

Nicholas investigated the availability of homesteads through the Dominion Lands Office in Winnipeg. They were available in the area, but they were even deeper into the Canadian Shield. He was told that there were surveyed homesteads available in the new province of Saskatchewan, and some Ukrainian speaking Austrians had already settled there. Nicholas pointed out to his brothers-in-law, Nick and Mike, the futility of trying to make a living in such unproductive land as that around Arbakka.

Mike related a story about his wife Domka, who, the previous fall, took her spade to a suitable garden spot. She dug down a few inches and struck a rock. Not an ordinary rock, she found, as she spaded around it; she was digging around the periphery of a veritable boulder! "I came up with a plan," Mike said. "Let's dig a space around it, and deeper, then we'll just shove the rock over into the void, fill soil over the top and you will have your garden plot.

"We worked like mules, and succeeded. Domka planted garlic in the soil we had scraped up to fill the void. In the spring, the garlic rose to the warming sun."

"'Wonderful,' Domka said, 'but the plants need water.' She watered them. The soil sank out of sight taking the garlic shoots with it."

They laughed, but the little anecdote brought out the realization that the Arbakka location would not provide a much better subsistence than life in their villages in Tovtri or Onut.

Nicholas Lazoruk, the eldest of the three, with Maria expecting a fourth child, was obligated to stay near home. Mike Lazoruk, and Nick Woronuk, volunteered to investigate the land around the community of Prince Albert in Saskatchewan. They would do this in the early spring. The die was set.

Erena had been prompting Nicholas to buy a violin. Thrilled that she so approved of his musical skill, he planned his trip back to the lumber camp by way of Winnipeg. The T. Eaton Company's main western store was there: a great Canadian enterprise that would serve a growing rural and urban population for more than a century.

Nicholas stopped at the store. Eaton's, as it was called in the vernacular throughout its long history, carried violins, and Nicholas perused the display, hanging on leather loops tied around the scrolls. "Beautiful, beautiful," he said under his breath, "but which one?" A clerk came to assist him and noticed the depth of veneration that the young man displayed as he gently held each violin and carefully plucked its strings.

Unconsciously, he tuned each one while he looked at another. His excellent sense of pitch, inherent in his memory, did not require a tuning fork; each string's resonant frequency was imprinted in his memory. The salesman stood back amazed. He had not seen anyone with this rare gift before. Clearly, an advanced violinist had come to buy an Eaton's instrument.

Nicholas plucked a brownish red instrument and hesitated. He plucked it again, and again, and the sounds it emanated fascinated him. He put the body of the instrument close to his left ear and plucked it once more. There was something unique about this one. It created a tone quality richer than the others he had tried. Only then did he look at the price tag attached to one of the pegs. His heart missed a beat. It was $10.00, and there was yet a bow and a case to add. It would amount to more than he was willing to spend. His face showed his distress, and the salesman acted on impulse.

"You buy this one and I will give you a bow and case to go with it for the same money," he said.

It was still a lot of money and beads of sweat formed on Nicholas's forehead. His hands shook and he felt a bit faint.

"Ten day work, too much," he replied with a shaky voice, his eyes downcast.

The salesman said, "You wait, I'll talk to the manager." He disappeared through the aisles. Nicholas picked a bow off the rack and drew a few notes. He retuned to the delicacy of sound the bow produced, and as he drew voices from the instrument, the manager and clerk returned. They stood a distance away, clearly impressed with the professional tones he created despite his amateur grasp of the violin and bow.

In keeping with the tradition that Eaton's had long established, the customer had to be satisfied. The manager offered the violin, the bow, and a case for $7.00. A week of work was worth it. Nicholas bought the package, and although reeling a bit from spending so much money, he knew that he would not part with this instrument for twice the amount.

He was an interesting sight to behold, walking into a lumber camp — a white sack on his back, now with a rope attached to sling it over his shoulders, an axe in one hand, and a violin case in the other. But

Nicholas was a complete man; he was married, had a son, a plan for the spring, and now a violin. Canada was indeed a great country.

Evenings, after a hard day's work, turned into musical adventures. Powerful sweating men pleaded that Nicholas play for them. As the days went by, his skills surpassed his own expectations. He remembered the tunes he had played as a child in Onut, for the pleasure of the villagers — but of concern to his grandfather. Now he could embellish the tunes with harmony from adjacent strings, a style and technique he had captured from the gypsy violinist in Budapest.

The men clapped their hands and stomped their feet. An occasional extrovert would add to the entertainment by clearing a space in the room and improvising a dance, adding to the merriment of all, including the fiddler. Nicholas was the most popular man in camp: uncannily skilled with his axe and equally skilled on the violin, he had found the way to associate with his fellow workers.

Nicholas made frequent visits home to see Erena and their new son, each time bringing his violin with him. He played, and little George, in his mother's arms, would stare at his father, transfixed. These were exciting visits, and it was always with reluctance that he left to return to camp.

When the winter's snow began to melt, Nicholas packed to leave. The night before he left camp, the men asked for yet another, and last, evening of music. His fiddle now sounded like two, from the harmonies he created by playing on more than one string at a time. This was a particularly boisterous evening — someone had brought bootleg liquor to generate an even more festive mood. As the bunkhouse rocked to stomping feet, clapping hands and the loud guffaws of half-drunk men, one passed his hat around for donations. Coins clanged one on top of the other, and the hat was handed to Nicholas and followed by a speech of appreciation from a man with a flushed face and slurred speech.

"Nick," he said, smacking his lips and wiping them on his sleeve, "you have kept us happy all win'er with your fiddle." He wiped his mouth again, and then continued, "Now you're leaving and we all will soon be going home too. But we will be back next win'er but you may be far away. Thank you, Nick, for the music and the fun we had. We will miss you and your wiolin."

For the first time, Nicholas heard his name contracted to Nick. It sounded good. He liked it. Everyone seemed to be called something abbreviated, if they were indeed friends: Joseph became Joe, Peter became Pete, and now Nicholas had become Nick. It was a nice convention, and he would hereafter refer to himself as Nick.

Later, he carefully counted the money that had been collected. It amounted to $5.50, more than three days work, and no deductions for food or lodging. The violin had nearly earned back its price already.

# CHAPTER 14

My uncle, Mike Lazoruk, had found employment across the border, working for a well-off farmer in Minnesota. He now quit his job too, and returned to Arbakka to join with Dad on their trip to Prince Albert. Dad refilled the sack that his mother had made in Onut, and Mike filled a flour sack that Domka had saved. They packed changes of clothing, extra work boots, several pairs of socks, and their sheepskin coats that they had brought from Bukovina. They said their good-byes, and with a feeling of confidence, left on the train.

They arrived in Prince Albert the following day. Looking at the heavy timber from the train window, they could see why this land was still not homesteaded. Clearing it to expose the soil beneath for farming would be a long and arduous task. They might even lose the homesteads: the Dominion Lands Act stipulated that forty acres had to be in production in three years.

They spent a day there and learned that a settlement area in the equally new province of Alberta, still had substantial land designated for homesteads north of Edmonton, They were committed to find better land; they re-boarded the train for Edmonton.

*Edmonton, in 1913, was a city in the midst of a boom. Its population had grown dramatically in the past few years. Construction of the High Level Bridge was nearing completion and it would connect the town of Strathcona, on the south side of the North Saskatchewan River, to Edmonton, on the north side. The two communities had amalgamated and Edmonton boasted a population of over 50,000 inhabitants. It had been chosen as the capital of the seven-year-old province and already had incorporated the University of Alberta.*

*Nick and Mike found the Government Lands Office and were directed northward, about 50 miles, to a site called Radway Centre, where homesteads had been surveyed. They walked a full hard day before they turned back — disillusioned. It was another heavily timbered area that would take years to clear and even longer to prepare it for seeding. Tired and disappointed, they returned to the land office in Edmonton for suggestions.*

*Now they were told that more new homestead land had been surveyed in a beautiful area in the Peace River Country. There was an access trail constructed to connect the villages of Edson and Grande Prairie. It would mean a 250-mile (350 km) walk to Grande Prairie from the railway station in Edson. To Nick it was exciting and challenging and could not be rejected. Mike showed a little reluctance, but agreed to go with his friend. They chose to go by train to Edson and then walk the Edson Trail to Grande Prairie.*

*To the two young men, hardened by years in lumber camps, the distant walk was not considered a major obstacle. Many others before them had already made the trek, and the employees at the land office were enthusiastic about the quality of the land that they would find.*

In 1913, Edson, Alberta, was a collection of log shacks spread haphazardly on a clearing, within sight of rugged mountains to the west. This was Nick's and Mike's first view of the Rocky Mountains, a reminder of the Carpathians they had left in Bukovina, but many times more majestic. The local landscape was one of rolling hills rising progressively westward where they blended into the towering

Rocky Mountains, whose snow covered peaks shimmered in the late April sunshine.

It was afternoon when they disembarked from the train onto the platform of the Edson station. The mountain air was clean and fresh, contrasting with the stuffy passenger car they had sat in for the past night and part of a day. Most passengers who left the train were men dressed in denim coveralls, wearing heavy boots, carrying cardboard boxes tied with course twine under one arm, and a fabric suitcase in the other. They too were young, perhaps, on average, a few years older than either Nick or Mike. It might have been the mountain air or the impending adventure that they were embarking on, but both men felt euphoric about the trail ahead of them and the land that they would find at its northern terminus.

A few men had just returned from the Peace River Country and shared their experiences with Nick and Mike. They said that most of the good homestead land around Grande Prairie had already been taken, and they would have to go another 30 or 40 miles in any direction they chose to find available land. They also told them what essentials they needed to make the trip: canvas for a lean-to shelter, a blanket for the night, and as much bread as they could pack. Beyond these, they would need 20 pounds of flour, some salt, a pot, a fry pan, a small caliber rifle to shoot small game for meat, and changes of clothes. Nick and Mike went to the little general store and bought the articles they needed to complete their requirements. They weighed their packs: 49 pounds each!

Then the storekeeper showed them backpacks that trappers always used. They found them more comfortable than carrying their load by hand. Each bought one and the salesman helped properly arrange their loads for optimum weight distribution. Each man also bought a small axe to carry in his hands.

The merchant spoke of trappers that returned every spring with furs that they loaded on the train for the Hudson's Bay Trading Post in Edmonton. He told Nick and Mike that the trappers were trustworthy, knew the trail well, and enjoyed company. For that reason, some built their cabins alongside the trail. But travelers, he warned, were strangers to the land and might be escaping the law. There were periodic patrols along the trail by the Northwest Mounted Police who sometimes brought these scoundrels back, their hands shackled behind their backs — but riding astride Government horses.

This businessman was talkative and persuasive. He was also fair; he did not attempt to overload these unseasoned land prospectors with stock that would increase their burden. He had seen many that had over-equipped themselves only to discard valuables along the trail or return to Edson, disillusioned and broke.

Stories had reached him of families that had set out on the trail and had never been heard from again. "Disappeared into the wilderness like smoke from a campfire," he described. The few years he had lived there, he had accumulated substantial histories of broken men and their broken dreams, all in the quest for the very land that Nick and Mike were seeking.

They took a room in the hotel, but the excitement of the coming morning did not bode well for a good night's sleep. They rose as the sun resurfaced after its dip below the horizon. Anxious to experience the trail, they delayed eating until they were hungry, and set out on a journey that had tested the stamina and will of the hardiest of men.

# CHAPTER 15

The little settlement of Edson seemed deserted of human life at this early hour. A mongrel barked, then rushed to meet them, its tail wagging from side to side, and its bark noisy but not aggressive. It brushed Mike's leg with its black fur, and he reached down to pet it while maintaining his pace. The animal looked upward at the men, trotted alongside for a few steps, suddenly found a scent that distracted it, and got left behind. The men chuckled at this display of fickleness; they turned to see it bounding back to its shack, with great leaps of joy. It had properly sent off the visitors and, at the same time, found something stimulating for its own senses.

The storekeeper had pointed to an opening cut into an almost opaque wall of trees north of his store. "That," he said, "is the Edson Trail. Follow it to a big lake — Sturgeon Lake — and then turn west, and it will take you to Grande Prairie." He said many men and a few women had returned and spoken of the trail conditions to him. The stories ranged from passable to impossible, depending on the season and the weather.

A rutted trail led to the opening in the timber. The men reached that point as the sun rose and began to warm the mountain air. The first few steps onto the trail would remain in their memories for all their lives. It would be the subject of recall over coffee or tea in their homes, as good neighbors passed idle time. A few strides further north, the low eastern sun suddenly disappeared behind towering evergreens that shrouded the trail into darkness. So dark, it seemed, that they had to pause momentarily until their eyes adjusted from the brilliant sunlight a few steps before. Looking a distance ahead, as through a tunnel, they could see light again.

The trail sloped gently upward, and a clearing appeared to the west with a patch of tall spring grass: an excellent pasture for their oxen, they concluded. If the trail were so endowed, the move in the fall would be easy. The oxen and cattle could graze, and the need for transporting much hay could be reduced.

Further along, the trail sloped downward, and at the valley bottom there was a little clear stream of spring run-off from the mountains. Both men dropped their pack boards and took out their pots, knelt by the bubbling stream and dipped into its crystal clear water for a drink.

They had walked only a few miles from Edson. The road ahead appeared suitable for wagons, although rolling and rutted throughout from settlers traveling it in the wet season. They sat for a few minutes, ate some bread, and took off their boots and socks to wade across the stream. The water was cold — very cold — but their feet were hot from the walk and the load they bore. Each man gasped when his feet submerged beneath the surface, then laughed at the shock, and continued. They picked their way across, stepping on rocks that protruded above the surface and braving the cold water where there was no alternative. The stream was only about ten steps across, and not more than a foot in depth. Crossing was no problem, and as they sat on the opposite side, pulling their socks over their wet feet, they talked about how easy it was to cross this first obstacle. Cooled feet, young hearts, and great hopes spurred them northward. They resumed their course along the Edson Trail.

By afternoon, they had crossed some areas of swamp that they had been told was *muskeg*, a term indigenous to the Cree of the northwest part of North America. The road builders had carefully laid poles across this bog, *corduroy* it was called, so that the animals and wagons would not sink into it. "Ingenious," said Nick, "we will have no problem crossing with our oxen and wagons if it's like this all the way."

Always the consummate optimist, it was Nick who had insisted on walking this trail with his somewhat reluctant brother-in-law, who might have been satisfied to return to Arbakka when the land at Radway showed little promise. This trait of his was to prove valuable in the days and months to come — not alone to complete this trek, but to survive the major challenges that were to follow.

By evening, they reached an area where the timber was thicker, but the trail remained without major obstacles. They were told of *Breakneck Hill* that they were approaching, a major challenge that wagon-drivers had to face. They had been climbing steadily upward from the valley below, and the occasional road markers nailed to the trees indicated their location as 30 miles.

They decided they had walked far enough this first day. There was a clearing to the right where they could take their sheet of canvas and tie it to two trees and peg the back flap to the ground. The area was strewn with dry branches to make a fire and a stream nearby for water: an ideal campsite. Though accustomed to walking, packing a weight of nearly 50 pounds was a new experience. Every muscle was aching.

If it were to rain, the sloped tarp would provide some cover. They built a fire, added dry lower branches of spruce, and packed water from the stream. Except for the quality of the tools they used, they had reverted to the primitive; these were the basic necessities of a camp for thousands of years. Tonight they mixed a healthy quantity of flour into the water, added some salt and a slip of salt pork, and cooked it into a bannock. It was a source of energy, but not flavor.

They talked about what Breakneck Hill might be like. The travelers with whom they had spoken in Edson described it simply and briefly — a site that should be recorded in history by the pioneers that crossed it: vague and confusing. Tomorrow they would see it. Then they slept.[3]

Morning arrived, and with it, the aches and pains of yesterday's long trek and heavy load. Each helped the other position his pack in place, and then they proceeded on the upward incline. The terrain was uneven: one knoll followed another, with some so steep as to present a challenge for oxen pulling a wagon. Several times they assumed the decline to be Breakneck Hill, but they could see that the trail continued to bring them upwards. Breakneck was said to begin at the highest point on the trail.

Looking down, they could see a large valley, beautiful in its green cover of spruce and pine. But between this panorama and where they stood was an obstacle that took their breaths away. "What is this?" Mike asked, "a kilometer from hell?"

"It's the bald pate of some giant prehistoric humanoid," Nick replied. "I think we are standing on a great archeological find!"

Breakneck Hill: its northern slope nearly bald of plant life; too steep, in places, to walk down without sidestepping; it continued for what appeared to be an endless distance before it disappeared around a bend.

It would present a stupendous challenge for oxen and wagon; in fact, it could lead to a disaster. They worked their way partway down to where they could see the bend and what appeared to be a scrap pile at the apex of its turn. Shaking their heads, they considered the system they would use to manage this slope.

"I don't know how we can manage with oxen and wagons," Mike began. "I don't see why they didn't cut the trail around this hill instead of going over it."

"Well, somehow others have made it, and if they could, we can too," Nick, confidant as usual, replied. "There is no question, we will get down the hill. Not sure in what condition, but we will get down," he quipped. "As to why they didn't go around this bald knoll, see the timber they would have had to cut? This was free! If they were paid by the mile, this way was easy money."

Mike's older brother, Nick, was experienced with draft animals, having worked on farms in Minnesota with horses and oxen. He would have ideas on how to manipulate this descent. It was procrastination; both knew it, and both subscribed to it. For the moment, it provided essential false comfort.

As they approached the curve, their eyes stared in disbelief. What they had spotted from above was a wrecked wagon and the carcasses of a team of dead horses. Hordes of blowflies were still feeding and breeding on their bloated remains. Scarcely thirty miles from Edson, some travelers had already met a challenge they could not overcome. It was the subject of much discussion between the two men as they made a cursory examination of the supplies scattered from the broken wagons and the harnesses still on the dead horses. It was a pathetic sight. "Surely," Mike said, "nothing further along the trail could be worse than this."

They pressed forward, frequently adjusting their packs to fresh areas where the web belt had not bruised the skin beneath. By noon they reached the Athabasca River. The water was murky with spring runoff and wagon tracks led along its gravel base. A small cable ferry took them across, their first experience with this form of travel.

They took off their heavy sheepskin coats and added them to the packs. Too late, they realized they should have left them in Edson with the storekeeper or the hotel. The warmth they provided was not needed during this time of year, and every pound of weight was an extra burden to contend with. The storekeeper was right, "…minimize the load because it could kill you sooner than anything on the trail." Occasionally, there were coats hanging on trees left by other travelers who had faced the same problem.

The trail began to deteriorate. Stumps from trees cut well above the ground surface protruded like little sentinels, warning adventurers without sufficient courage to reconsider their decision to go further. They saw the wagon tracks that wove around these obstacles, and they knew they would have to do the same.

Progress had slowed; their shoulders were raw from the rubbing of the web pack straps. They took their packs off for short distances, carrying them in one hand and the axe in the other. But 50 pounds in one hand soon caused their rib cage to ache. They shouldered their packs again, grimacing as the straps bore on the bruised skin beneath.

That evening they spotted a trapper's cabin just off the road. They heeded the storekeeper's advice; fatigued and hungry they knocked on the door. It opened instantly, and before them stood a man, bearded and unkempt, with a smile that radiated from ear to ear, clearly expressing his joy for the gift of their company. He invited them in, and his first words were, "You must be hungry." Without waiting for an answer he moved the teapot to the center of the potbellied stove and threw an extra stick into the firebox.

Before they had a chance to speak, he rambled on for some time about his family, far away, and the number of Americans seeking land

"…up there on the Peace." When Nick finally had a chance to speak, the lonely trapper slowed his effervescent monologue. He realized that these two understood only one or two of his words out of ten. Most of his running dialogue had missed its mark.

However, his generosity was unaffected. He reached behind a stool and withdrew a pot, still warm from his dinner a few hours before; it contained leftovers from a rabbit he had cooked. The meat was soon reheated and potatoes boiled. Nick and Mike shared with him some of their bread that they had bought in Edson.

Three men, in a cabin no more than 8 feet square, speaking two completely different languages, still found a way to be generous to each other. It was an inspiring event, and the memory of it would be recalled many times in the future.

Hides were piled in stacks on the floor, and others were hanging on the walls in various stages of drying. Between these, the two strangers made their beds. A trapper's cabin, they found, was significantly more comfortable that the lean-to the night before. More tired than ever, Mike and Nick slept a little later into the morning. The trapper, however, was up at first light, and had brought water from a nearby stream…and another rabbit that had recklessly crossed his path. He split a few blocks of wood, and the pounding of the axe roused the two visitors from their beds.

The morning meal was rabbit stew and wild spring berries of a type unknown to the guests. They asked the trapper if they might leave their sheepskin coats with him until they returned some weeks later. He admired the coats. On the inside, the tanned hides were beautifully hand stitched together, a technique not commonly used in North America. The coats were reversible, so that the sheep wool could either be worn on the inside or out. "Of course you can leave them here. I'll store the coats for you, and you can pick them up when you return to Edson," he said.

Their load was perceptively lighter without the coats. They bid farewell to the trapper, who seemed to have forgotten about their limited English and continued to ramble on, even as they turned to face north and proceed on their way.

For the next five days the trail was never impassible, but progressively narrower, and the workmen who had cut it no longer corduroyed the muskeg. Some of the bogs were lengthy, and both men carried thin poles to test the depth of the brown muck before each step. They had abandoned removing their boots and socks because the opaque water covered countless snags that would have torn the skin from a bare foot. Progress was slow, but remained steady.

Nick and Mike made mental notes of these areas and discussed how they would need to guide the oxen and wagons to successfully cross them. Unfamiliar with the vagaries of foothills weather, the men thought that the snowmelt was the water source that had caused these bogs. By fall, they assumed, these areas would have dried up, making them easier to negotiate.

By the ninth day they were running short of food. The mile markers showed that they had not yet traveled 180 miles. Little flour remained, the salt pork was gone, though rabbits would fill that need, and the bread was moldy. Reaching Sturgeon Lake was now their primary focus. The Natives there lived on fish, they were told, and Nick and Mike craved something other than rabbit. It was another two days walk, and there would be only bits of bannock and rabbit meat to eat. It seemed there was always a stream nearby. Fortunately, water was plentiful.

There were occasional stopping places: cabins and barns built to provide shelter and comfort for travelers and their animals. When these places happened to coincide with their plan to rest, they used them. However, those past the midpoint on the trail were not stocked with staff or provisions.

Before reaching Sturgeon Lake, the last of the flour was used. They realized they should have been more prudent with their food intake, and the plan that they would be in Grande Prairie in ten days was incorrect. It was now going to take thirteen days.

To their advantage, the pack weight had lessened and their shoulders calloused. With their food nearly gone, they packed only their axes and a few pounds in the pack: the fry pan and pot, some tea, their blanket, and changes of clothes. Nearing civilization brightened their spirits, and although weak, their pace quickened with each mile they covered.

The blue water of Sturgeon Lake appeared through the branches of the trees. Their hope of restocking their food supply was foremost on their minds. They were anxious to find an Indian settlement to buy some fish and vegetables. An encampment of teepees in a cove of the lake a mile away could be seen; they followed the lakeshore to the settlement.

The Indians were friendly and did sell fish to them, but either they had no vegetables or were unable to understand the requests. They wanted to exchange the fish for liquor, but the men carried none. They agreed, reluctantly, on cash, and brought out both raw and dried fish. Nick and Mike bought some of each. That night they made camp, totally fatigued and ravenously hungry; but their spirits improved now that there was something other than rabbit meat to eat.

The following day they crossed the Smoky River on a cable ferry operated by a skilled Metis ferryman, and a day and a half later they saw the tiny settlement of Grande Prairie ahead of them. The road was now only slightly rutted, even better than they had encountered on the first day out of Edson.

The hotel in Grande Prairie was a log building with a few rooms for travelers, a small restaurant, but no running water or indoor toilets. Still, to Nick and Mike, it was a quantum leap forward from the facilities they had used for the past weeks on the trail. First they ate, and drank real coffee, then washed up and relaxed on the bed — a real bed — with a spring filled mattress, albeit worn, with several springs penetrating its cover. A coal oil lamp lit the room that night, but they did not leave it lit for long. They were soon asleep.

They awoke early to a bright morning, the sun already warming the air and land, encouraging the grain fields to grow. They ate breakfast quickly, and then walked to the Dominion Lands Office to inquire about the availability of homesteads in the area. Several men were standing outside waiting for the office to open. The door swung open. They would soon know where good land could be obtained, and if their exhausting trip was worth it.

The Dominion Lands Office in Grande Prairie, a log building that served as a registry office for those who were making application for homestead land, also provided advice and guidance on identifying survey markers. When the two men were able to discuss homesteads with the officials, they were told that previous waves of settlers had taken up all the surveyed land around Grande Prairie. Another substantial area had been surveyed and was available in the Spirit River area, some 50 miles farther north. The land was described as totally free of rocks, sparsely wooded, with the Spirit River providing a fine water supply. The trail to the area was good and there was only one small river to negotiate. They were given the survey coordinates of unassigned land, and Mike and Nick immediately filled their pack sacks with food and pushed northward to the Spirit River.

# CHAPTER 16

The name choice for the village of Grande Prairie was appropriate. It was situated on a grand prairie with nearly complete quarter sections void of dense timber. Plots had been seeded to oats, and these plots enthused the two men. They were thick with stubble from last fall's harvest, and showed potential for superb crop production — a remarkable contrast to the wasteland of Arbakka. By now, Nick and Mike were ecstatic. Their pace quickened and they reached the Spirit River in a comparatively easy two days hike.

Finding the survey markers was not difficult. The survey crews had outlined townships, sections, and quarter sections by clearing narrow trails between the stakes that defined the particular plot. Water was a key consideration, and the Spirit River did, in fact, provide a fine source of water.

They followed the river, and Nick was the first to identify his choice for a homestead quarter section, and adjoining his, he selected another for his father. The men agreed that the next river lot, as it was called, would be for Nick Lazoruk, and adjoining it to the north, was for Mike to file on. The great trek had yielded results. Both pioneers were over-joyed with the quality of the land, the river, and the occasional patches of open area ready for plowing, with only some willow bush to clear. Indeed, they teased, this is where Eden was situated in the first place.

But there was yet one hurdle to overcome: they had to be the first to enter their names on the application forms for their selected sites. Hundreds of homesteaders were spilling out from Grande Prairie to the west and north, filing on any surveyed plot they chose, and it was a race against this element that they had to win. They set their course south, back to Grande Prairie, to fill out their homestead applica-tions, arriving late at night and finding the Land Office closed. They made their beds right against its door, determined to be the first in the morning to gain entrance and secure their homesteads.

They were awake long before the agents came, but shortly after they were up, more men appeared with the same objective: to be early in line. By the time the office doors opened there were a dozen men waiting and more arriving. The population of the village seemed less than the number of people waiting at the agent's door.

Good fortune! No one had filed on the lands they had selected, and with the help of one of the agents, they filled out the forms appropri-ately, spent most of their remaining money for the $10.00 registration fee per file, and overjoyed, went to restock their supplies for the hike back to Edson.

Groceries in Grande Prairie were nearly double the price in Edson, which, in turn, were nearly double the cost of the same purchases in Edmonton. When they completed stocking supplies, they knew they would not have money enough to buy tickets back to Winnipeg. They would have to find work. That did not seem to matter; although they missed their wives and children, they had homesteads. Planning how they would sell their properties in Manitoba and rent railway cars to haul their possessions to Edson was the topic of conversation as they retraced their tracks. From here on it would be relatively easy — they thought.

They made better time returning to Edson. Following a week of dry weather, the muskeg was firmer, the covering muck not so deep, and they knew better where to walk. They stopped at the trapper's cabin to retrieve their sheepskin coats, but the trapper was gone, and so were the coats. Since the furs were gone too they presumed he had gone into Edson to take the train to Edmonton to sell his furs. Nick and Mike were upset because the coats were much warmer than the felt fabric ones that locals wore in winter. There was the possibility that they would retrieve their possessions in the fall when they came through with their families. The return trip to Edson took 10 days, and they had adequate provisions.

The railway needed workers on their extra gangs and the men found work immediately. Both had experience in this type of work in Manitoba, and although menial and dirty, the pay was good. To earn enough for train fare took them two months, but finally they were able to buy tickets and return to Arbakka.

For both men, the return home was glorious. Little George was now crawling and had grown considerably. Erena was overjoyed to have her family together again. Nick had been away for nearly three months, but he had land, beautiful black soil without rock. "There is a building site that is already clear except for a willow bush or two, and near it are thick straight trees from which to build a log house, and water — a running stream with a year-round water supply, less than a hundred yards from the clearing," Nick explained excitedly.

He told of the garden soil, and Erena's heart began to race. Vegetables, fruits, and herbs that she would be able to grow next year, created a vision of a panorama of gardens flashing before her eyes.

The last lush gardens that she had seen were in Tovtri over a decade ago. Nick could see her excitement and he embellished his description with metaphors. He told of the gardens that they had seen: potato plants with leaves like elephant ears, carrots, onions all growing twice or more times as tall as in Manitoba. Erena could hardly wait.

When they told of the wonders of the Peace Country to Steve Chalus, a brother-in-law to Erena, he immediately chose to sell out in Arbakka and join the group.

The Lazoruk brothers and Steve Chalus needed to harvest their meager crops, and sell what they could, including the land for the improvements they had made. Unlike Nick Woronuk, who had not taken a homestead in Manitoba, but had worked at various jobs and had saved money, the other families on this migration had little cash but did have assets to convert.

*Dad had not been a farmer, although he had some seasonal experience working for farmers, and, of course, he had spent some time with Uncle John and gotten some understanding of draft animals and farm equipment. He bought a one-bottom walking plow, three harrows, and a wagon. With the excellent oxen and cow he and Mother already owned, he was as equipped as he needed to be to begin cultivating land in the Spirit River Settlement. This group would initiate the first dedicated grain farming operation in the area.*

*During these early years there were two Spirit River communities: The hamlet of Spirit River, about six miles west of their homesteads, and Spirit River Settlement, about two miles to the southwest which consisted of two small stores and little else. The Settlement would later be renamed; meantime, the Revillion and Calkin stores served the basic needs of the homesteaders.*

It was an exciting and busy summer. Within a month, there was property to sell, the railway to negotiate for two boxcars to have spotted on a sidetrack, hay to prepare, gardens to harvest, and multiple other obligations to fulfill before they could leave. The hay for the oxen was the first priority. The pastureland that they had seen a short distance from Edson didn't reappear until a few miles from Sturgeon Lake. Feed would be needed for most of the trail. They mowed and dried their hay crop, then selected only the best for the oxen, and had it machine pressed to minimize the space it would occupy. It became clear to the group that their four wagons would not be able to haul their personal essentials and adequate feed for the animals.

The Sandul family, cousins to the Lazoruks, had an eighteen-year-old son who asked to go with the group to file for homesteads for his father and himself. They needed a fifth wagon and driver — perhaps they would be able to use him to drive one wagon. Young Fred Sandul was overjoyed; it offered the adventure the youth sought. He immediately agreed for food and travel expenses.

The community of Arbakka was indifferent or, in some cases, showed hostility to their move. Most residents were eking out a living by working all winter in lumber camps or for established farmers in Minnesota. A little money was being saved and that was insignificantly more than they would have accomplished in Austria. This idea of moving to an unsettled area, living with tribes of *Indians*, who were likely still fuming over the fate of Louis Riel, seemed imprudent. Such concerns contrasted with the restless character of Nick Woronuk. Young Fred Sandul also felt that this idea was not rational, but participating in the adventure was irresistible. His parents were pleased. A fifth wagon was purchased and oxen were provided to pull it.

Since the plan to explore for better land was initiated in the fall of 1912, Nick Woronuk and Mike Lazoruk could not attend church. When the decision was made to move, none of the families had time for church services. Their time was directed to preparations for their new venture. Having grown up under the umbrella of the Greek

Orthodox faith, they were strongly religious, but a few were beginning to question some of its dogma.

The church taught that members of the congregation would support each other during times of need. None of the unrelated members showed any inclination to help these families, rushing to pack to make the move before winter set in. Perhaps they were envious. In their present state on the Laurentian rocks, all were destitute and would always remain so unless the hand of God miraculously improved their lot. A few, including Nick's brother Simon and his family, had already returned to Bukovina.

There was, however, a sense of community in Arbakka. With this migration of four families, their absences in church were factors that changed the dynamics of the settlement, and contributed to the dismissive attitude by those who chose to remain.

As fall approached, the usual communal assistance to the departing families remained conspicuously absent. The church, so vocal in promoting cooperation amongst its adherents, was silent. No preacher appeared on their doorsteps; no words of encouragement, blessing, or caution were uttered. Instead, there was total disengagement. The four families sensed this change profoundly, but there was little time to dwell on it. All had been active church members and most had played a part in the construction of the first Greek Orthodox Church in Canada.

They had agreed to pay a fee of $3.00 per year to support a priest who travelled from Minnesota monthly to conduct services such as marriages, baptisms, and funerals. Otherwise, Sunday services were held with lay ministers from the congregation including, on occasion, one of the four departing male members.

While struggling to load their boxcars, a man in a long black coat, black hat, and a beard approached. Mike Lazoruk recognized him immediately; he was the preacher, of Russian Orthodox persuasion, who came from Minnesota. He came directly to Mike and said, "Metro, you and Nicholai each owe me $3.00."

"And what do I owe you $3.00 for, Pastor?" Mike replied.

"You haven't paid your dues for a year," came the reply.

"But Pastor, I have been away most of the year, searching for a better land, because you know, as well as I, that we cannot survive on this land," Mike responded.

"You still owe me $3.00, and I have come a long way to collect from you and Nicholai."

"Well, I'll tell you what," Mike argued, "you go to Nicholai, and if he pays you, I will too."

He left Mike and went to Nick.

"Nicholai," he addressed, "you and Metro each owe me $3.00. Metro says if you pay, he will also pay. Pay me the $3.00 before you leave Arbakka."

"But Pastor," replied Nick, "what on earth do I owe you the money for?"

"For what the church has done for you; for what I have done for you," the Pastor replied haughtily.

"But you know as I do, Pastor, that this past year the church has done nothing for me. There has not been anyone to help me in this work. I have had to do it by myself." He continued in Mike's manner, "but if Metro pays, I will pay too."

Now clearly upset, the pastor returned to Mike and told him what Nick had said, and then reminded Mike that if they should get in some financial difficulty in the new settlement, he would collect donations from the church and send it to whoever needed help.

"And how will you send it?" Mike asked. "There are 300 miles of bush and muskeg. How will the money get to me?"

At this, the pastor lost all control, and with lips tightened he turned to Nick Lazoruk and Steve Chalus and in a subdued tone, said:

"Nick Lazoruk and Steve Chalus, you have paid your dues to me in church while your brother and brother-in-law were away. May you have a fortunate trip, and may the grace of God follow you on your road." Leveling his eyes at the other two, he continued, but with venom in his voice, "And you, Nicholai Woronuk, and you, Metro Lazoruk, may you be doomed, and never reach your destination, never return, and may you be struck by lightning!"

With these words, he strode away, taking huge steps, "…as if he was walking on the hot coals of hell," Mike said. He disappeared amongst the railways cars, having just sown the seeds of a fracture with the Orthodox faith in four families who, for years, were in good standing in his parish.

*The five families who made the trek along the Edson-*
*Grande Prarie Trail left to right:*

*Nicholas and Erena Woronuk (nee Lazoruk) holding George (1)*

*Yakiw and Wasylena Lazoruk, parents of the married brothers and sisters*

*Stephan and Elena Chalus (nee Lazoruk) and son William (5)*

*Nickolai, holding Steve (2) and Maria Lazoruk (nee Korol), holding*
*Alyce (6 months), Lena (6) in back and Dora (3) in front*

*Metro (Mike) and Domka (Dora) Lazoruk (nee Rosko),*
*holding Dolly (3) and Sadie (5) behind Lena*

*Not pictured: Onufry (Fred) Sandul (18), nephew and*
*cousin who drove the ox team for Yakiw Lazoruk*

*Taken in Stuartburn, Manitoba in 1913 just prior to their*
*departure for the Peace River Country of Alberta*

# CHAPTER 17

The spur rail line, from Vita, Manitoba, would bring them to Winnipeg where the two freight cars would link to the Canadian Northern Railway. It would pull them westward through the Province of Saskatchewan and into Edmonton, Alberta. Winnipeg had experienced a phenomenal growth since the women in the group had passed through it on the way to their homes-to-be in Arbakka. Erena remembered the city as the filthiest place she had ever imagined in 1903 when the Lazoruk family first arrived and spent a few days in provisional immigrant quarters there. At that time, the city was experiencing a second influx of settlers on their way west to homesteads or to start businesses. In the next ten years, Winnipeg had experienced a 70% annual growth rate. The women, remembering it as a small city of 40,000, now saw it reaching 160,000.

They had time to go shopping while the train cars were switched to tracks that would take them to Edmonton. Erena, Maria, Domka, and Elana and their children walked into the city to shop for the basic essentials for life in the remote land where they would be living. The prices were unbelievably low, and Erena bought a coffee grinder, a large copper boiler washtub and various pots and pans that she did not yet possess. The quality of the kitchenware was excellent for its day; most of her purchases were still in use 40 years later.

They were a spectacle to see: four women each packing a child on one arm and an array of pots, pans, and silverware on the other. Erena carried George and the copper boiler, inside which rattled several other kitchen utensils. But they laughed about the image they portrayed, and were overjoyed with the purchases that would serve them in the future. This was Erena's first outing without Nick, and the first time she had ever bought with her husband's money, independent of his approval. Her purchases would prove to be invaluable on the trail and on the homestead.

The men, meanwhile, walked the oxen. The animals, unfamiliar with trains, showed some trepidation to re-enter the boxcars, but with persistent urging, these placid animals climbed the ramps and took their places, squeezed tight, one against the other.

To reach Edmonton took three days. The fall weather was warm; the women and children rode in the passenger car along with alternating men (one man rode in each boxcar to care for the animals). The train stopped about every 6 hours and the men carried buckets of water for the stock and rearranged access to hay. These animals were tied up short, so they had scarcely room to take a single step. Nick kidded that there was no room in the boxcars to pack even an extra fry pan!

The Lazoruk family was complete in this move; two sisters, Elana Chalus and Erena Woronuk, and two brothers, Nick and Mike Lazoruk, along with parents Yakiew and Wasylena Lazoruk, meant that the entire family that had left Bukovina in 1903 had now left Manitoba for better prospects in Alberta.

It was September 5, 1913, when the train's whistle signaled the arrival in Edson. The clanging of steel on steel, the squeal of brakes, and the blasts of steam from the engine brought the train to a halt. The train ride was over. It would be the last train they would hear for three years.

Railway building was big business then. Companies were being formed to build lines feeding into the transnational networks to the West Coast established by the southerly route of the Canadian Pacific Railway through Calgary, and the northern route, the Canadian Northern Railway, through Edmonton. Numerous lines were planned or being constructed, radiating from Edmonton to serve areas where farmers had established themselves and would soon have grain to ship and supplies to buy.

The Government of Alberta authorized the construction of a railroad to the Peace River Country. It would serve the areas on the north side of the Peace River and the south side. Utilization of the Edson Trail was intended to last only until the rail had reached Grande Prairie, or some location near homesteads. Settlers would then be able to ship their produce, and pay the freight charges. That market would create a return on investment to the railway companies.

This contingent of pioneers knew that rail would be coming to their area; it was, in fact, a major incentive for settlement. By 1913, immigrants from many countries in Europe were being encouraged to file for homesteads where they could become grain farmers, and the railways would take their grain on the first leg of its journey to markets all over the world. They had to move now, settle and begin clearing land and build dwellings, in order to satisfy the requirements of the Dominion Lands Act. The Act stipulated that within three years, their improvements on the homestead would be assessed, and if they met the requirements of the Act, the homesteader would receive full title to that quarter section of land. This group hoped to meet those stipulations and to have grain for market when the railway reached their area.

Once their boxcars were spotted on a sidetrack in Edson, they commenced unloading. Four men, and the youthful Fred Sandul, pitched into the task with vigor, fueled by excitement. Next morning they would form a five-team wagon train, each drawn by oxen. Behind each wagon, cinched by a lead rope, was a milk cow, an invaluable animal that assured the key nutrients for each family's children.

For their personal needs, each family had a tent, a two burner cast-iron wood heater, several lengths of stove pipe, some pots and pans, utensils, and the garden produce that they had collected in Manitoba. Potatoes were picked earlier than optimum, driven by the realization that winter would be setting in earlier in Northern Alberta than in Southern Manitoba. Their supplies were carefully calculated to last two weeks, or a day or two more, in order to reach Grande Prairie. By fall, they predicted, the muskeg on the trail should have dried, or nearly so. This wrong prediction was based on the experience Mike and Nick noted: the muskeg was significantly less troublesome on their return trip in the spring, after just a week of dry weather.

Erena Woronuk, the youngest woman on the trip, not yet nineteen years old, saw the lush gardens around some of the homes in Edson. Even with the town's proximity to the craggy Rocky Mountains to the west, the soil was rich, and the gardens, just being picked, were luxuriant with produce. Her heart beat faster; although there were a few rocks, compared to Arbakka, they were insignificant. Nick had assured her he did not find a single rock on the lands he registered. "Nick," she teased, "I warn you; if I find a rock in my garden, I'll throw it at you!"

Maria Lazoruk, the tiniest of the four women, already with four children, the youngest still too young to walk, had to be the wonder woman of all time. Her acquiescent nature was a marvel for all to observe. She set a tone of amenability, an essential in the grueling times to come.

Domka Lazoruk's personality contrasted with Maria. Strong willed and outspoken, remarkably talented in crafts, she was, nevertheless, obstinate and had the capacity to create havoc. But this trait would prove invaluable when the going got tough. She was loyal to the core, unrelenting in her drive, and would succeed where others might have failed. With two small children in hand — and pregnant with her third — she had an extra burden to bear, but her drive would prove ceaseless, and she did succeed.

Elana Chalus, the eldest of the Lazoruk children, possessed an unlimited trait of kindness and, like Maria, but unlike Domka, acquiesced to the demands of her husband to the point of servitude. Her faith in God and His works were the constant she relied upon. Throughout her life, she would accept her condition, regardless how tragic it may have seemed to others, as God's gift to her. It was not subject to complaint or argument; it was a simple fact of life.

Wasylena Lazoruk, 54 years old, the mother of two sons and two daughters on this escapade into the wilderness, was a mix of the religious servitude of Elana, the idealistic Erena, and the good nature of sons Nick and Mike. Tall and slender, strong in will and physique, and possessing an unquestioning faith in the works of God, she was, and would remain, an adhesive that kept the four families focused on their objective.

Yakiew, Wasylena's husband, 75 years old, already weakened by age and years of unrelenting toil, was tall — but frail. He would be incapable of adding an appreciable component of strength to the tasks of loading freight and preparing for the journey. But he would hold up his end later, when travel was punishing, and the stronger men were reaching their limits of endurance.

Nicholas Woronuk (Nick), twenty three, was vivacious, handsome, intelligent, and a visionary. It was he who persuaded his in-laws to abandon their hopeless situation in Arbakka, and though an inexperienced farmer, he was determined to find a location where there was hope in the future for prosperity. He felt an intense responsibility for the success of this venture to lands isolated from what the group knew as civilization. He was remarkably strong for his smaller stature and seemingly impossible to fatigue. His personality would bode well when their travel got difficult. He found humor and nonsense, both traits he had used even before he left his village of Onut, an indispensable morale booster throughout the hardships awaiting them. In his wagon, carefully stashed in the hay, he buried his violin.

Nick Lazoruk was a physical contrast to Nick Woronuk. This Lazoruk was tall and raw-boned, twenty five, with handsome, distinctive features that he passed on to his enlarging family. He was quieter than his talkative brother-in-law, sincere, and profoundly generous. Nick had much experience with both oxen and horses where he had worked in Minnesota. The group depended on his expertise, in this case with oxen, to coax from them strength and obedience even beyond their inherent nature. His skills would be called upon on several occasions that were critical to the success of the venture.

Mike Lazoruk, twenty four, was, by stature, a man like Nick Woronuk. He was short but not as stalky, kind, more talkative than his brother, and because of their trip together over the Edson Trail earlier in the year, he had become a close and personal friend of Nick Woronuk. What extraversion he might have possessed did not become evident, living in the shade of his wife, Domka, who dominated over him like an umbrella to bright sunlight. But for his lesser stature, he more than held up his end. He would tire, but recover readily; extreme exertion was clearly more trying for him than for the other men.

Steve Chalus was an enigma. His stature was no larger than Nick Woronuk, but his strength was superhuman. His disposition was arrogant, unquestionably so, demanding his wife Elana to carry out work equivalent to his own. Steve Chalus was a survivor. If anyone were going to survive this trip it would be he. He drove his oxen with the same characteristic he displayed to every living thing around him: it would serve his needs or be thrashed into submission. He was brave, if not foolhardy; risks were simply factors in life that determination and physical strength would overcome. He would be tested on the trail, and because of his dogged determination, they would all succeed.

Fred Sandul was a strapping young man with a keen sense of adventure. Not yet highly skilled as an oxen driver, he did do his job without complaint and was an important contributor to the manpower necessary to manage on the trail. He was a first cousin to the Lazoruk family, remarkably jovial and talkative throughout the time with them. His contribution of driving the fifth wagon was critical. Without the extra load of hay he carried, they would not have managed to keep the oxen alive. Without their animals, the consequences to the families would have been disastrous.

The children, of whom there were eight, ranged in age from Lena, the oldest at six, to the youngest, her sister Alyce, at six months. Between these two were six others, of ages five, three, two, and one. Each woman was responsible for the welfare of a child, but Domka had two and Maria had four. Only Maria could survive the task of looking after four, and she did, without uttering a single word of complaint.

Bulky farm equipment created a problem. When the tons of hay and the necessary supplies for human survival were loaded on the wagons, along with sleighs for later winter travel, there was no remaining space for a single piece of farm machinery. Nick Woronuk, whose English skills were better than the others, was delegated to inquire where the equipment could be stored until winter. They would return with sleighs and bring the equipment to their homesteads. He approached the blacksmith in the largest building in Edson. Good fortune prevailed; for a small fee of a few dollars the shop was able to store the equipment until they returned.

They set up their tents in darkness that first night, cooked a decent meal, discussed their plans for the morning, and went to bed. It was exciting; none had set up a tent before, and none of the women had cooked on a camp stove. But it worked out better than expected. They would become experts in these tasks before long.

# CHAPTER 18

*Map showing the approximate route of the Edson-Grande Prairie Trail of 1913.*

There was stirring in the camps before sunrise. Fires were stoked in the stoves and the women were preparing a morning meal. Crushed wheat cereal was boiled until it gelled into porridge, then sugared slightly and covered with whole milk fresh from their cows. It was

129

a healthy and substantial breakfast. All the children were fed in the same way except Alyce. Too young to digest such coarse food, she still fed from her mother's breast. George Woronuk, then a one-year-old toddler just beginning to walk, was fed cereal too, but supplemented with milk and bread.

At daybreak, the children, oscillating between alert and asleep, could not be cuddled as they had become accustomed to. They would whimper and lie down on the ground wherever they were and sleep another few winks. The women bustled, washing and packing the utensils while the men began to break down the camp. As the rising sun began to show its colors in the eastern sky, the wagon train was ready to move to the opening in the forest to the north of Edson.

Because Nick Woronuk's oxen were one of the stronger teams and he knew the trail, he was elected to lead the procession. Nick Lazoruk, then Steve Chalus, then Fred Sandul and Mike Lazoruk followed him. Each family's cow was tied to the tailgate of a wagon. Yakiew and Wasylena sat with Fred Sandul whose load was the lightest and his experience the least. Scattered to broken cumulous clouds had gathered overnight, but the morning sun seemed bright and inviting. There was banter between the wagons, and careful attention was paid to the children nestled in the hay. The rough trail to the bush awakened them, and the older ones were playing in the hay, pushing their hands in as far as they could, trying to touch another's hands below the surface. When they reached the forest opening, the sun was just above the eastern horizon. It was beautiful, warming the adult travelers, now comfortably seated on the wagon seats, nearly two meters above the ground.

The lead oxen did not need urging to move forward at a good pace. The teams behind faithfully followed the team ahead ... no problems. In his rear position, Mike Lazoruk noticed that when the lead team entered the opening in the forest, the official beginning of the Edson-Grande Prairie Trail, the team and wagon disappeared into the shadows. They were now on the trail to their homesteads. Young, strong, and excited, they could not wait to get started on what they planned as a two-week excursion. Nick Woronuk whistled a few tunes for his son, who paused from his playful mood in his mother's arms, to listen. The skill was incisive and the intonation precise. Nick Woronuk was an entertainer with his whistling.

Even young eyes took a few minutes to adjust to the difference in sunlight and darkness that the forest presented. The wagon wheels struck occasional stumps and roots jarring the passengers and nearly throwing them off their perches. But the driver's eyes soon adjusted to the shadows, and the men steered the oxen carefully. As the day progressed, the oxen seemed to learn to avoid such obstacles, easing the driver's responsibility.

The euphoria of entering the trail eventually passed, and Nick Woronuk, like Mike Lazoruk, began considering the maneuvers they had planned for descending Breakneck Hill. They remembered the rubble at the turn near the bottom, the dead and decaying horses that they had seen on their walking trip to the Peace River Country. They wondered if the braking system they had considered would be sufficient to hold the wagons from overrunning the oxen, spooking them and ending up in the heap like the other wagon before them. When they stopped for lunch and to rest and feed the animals, they discussed their concerns. Nick Lazoruk suggested he would lead the oxen down to give them confidence, holding them in line with the wagon pole. It was a comforting thought: another device to overcome the challenge that they would face tomorrow.

The sun had passed overhead and the shadows now began to creep from the southwest. Time was passing and the children were getting restless, hungry, and chronically thirsty. The forest was denser now, and the trail became steeper in its inclines. Nick and Mike remembered these slopes; they were approaching Breakneck Hill. An hour later they reached the apex of the climb and Nick stopped his oxen. Sitting on top of the wagon, the slope of the hill looked more precipitous than it had standing on the ground. How were they to negotiate this drop? Even the suggestion made by Nick Lazoruk, that he would lead the oxen downward, seemed inadequate. There was serious risk for a man in front and for the driver on the driving perch of the wagon — a risk of injury or even death. Nick Lazoruk got off his wagon to survey the notorious hill that had claimed animals, possessions, and, who knew, perhaps some human lives as well. He walked down the slope a few steps, enough to see its incline, so steep that he was forced to make heel pockets with his boots to prevent sliding out of control.

Nick knew oxen, knew that they were the most placid of draft animals, sure-footed, and trustworthy, but once frightened, they were unstoppable. Somewhat like bison, they were capable of stamped-ing. He worried that if the first wagon hurtled, that message would somehow reach the other beasts, and they could lose their entire wagon train. When he observed the tracks made by earlier travelers, he noticed a third rut between the two wheel ruts. Obviously, not only were the wheels blocked from turning, but others had also dragged an anchor of some kind to further control the rate of descent.

It struck him — previous travelers were dragging a log as an extra brake. He had the answer. They would cut five substantial trees of a length they could physically manage, and trim the branches with short stubs remaining. He would still lead the oxen, from the side, giving them confidence from his gentle voice and encouraging tone. They would put a limb through the spokes of both front and back wheels to prevent them from turning, and unhitch the cow. They would attach a log to the back of each wagon, with its tip rearward, to maximize the resistance to sliding that such an arrangement would produce. Two men would be assigned to keep the log straight as it was pulled downhill and, step by step, they would descend. That was the plan. Next morning they would put it to the test.

They made camp near the top of Breakneck Hill. It had been a long day, the oxen needed rest, the wives had to prepare food, and the men had to cut logs. It was well after dark when they finished their tasks. Tired, but anxious about their improvisations to make descent successfully, they slept, but restlessly.

The clouds that were gathering the day before were denser in the morning. There was the distinct threat of rain, and that would make the slope more treacherous. The men were anxious to make the descent before the weather worsened. The incline to the top had brought them to a height of nearly a mile above sea level, higher than any had experienced in their lifetimes. There was coolness in the morning air, a forewarning that nature provides when winter is imminent. The men hurried to tie the logs to the wagons. Nick Woronuk would make the descent first. His oxen were the most stoical. They hoped to learn much from this first attempt that they could apply to the others. Erena, carrying George, began to work her way carefully along the edge of the slope where trees grew, and she could support herself with their trunks and branches. Nick Lazoruk grasped the halter of the left ox and Nick Woronuk took the reins to walk beside the wagon rather than ride on it. Fred Sandul and the powerful Steve Chalus were assigned to guide the log behind, holding on to the stubs of branches that were left longer and protruded upward for that purpose. Mike and Yakiew Lazoruk were left with the other teams and cattle to keep them from following the lead team.

They descended over the crest of the hill and stopped to push the braking poles through the spokes of the front and hind wheels and then resumed their long slide downhill. Nick Lazoruk maintained a constant low voice dialogue with the animals. Although their eyes were dilated wide from fear, Nick had the capacity to gain their trust, and they followed him as a child would a parent into dangerous waters.

Watching this procession from the side, Erena could not help but gasp at what she was seeing. At times the slope was so steep that it appeared to her that the wagon was balancing on its front wheels, but Nick Lazoruk's constant re-assuring tone seemed to hypnotize the animals, and step-by-step, they made the descent. Steve and Fred noticed that the trunk they were guiding followed the rut made by other similar arrangements before them, and they were using the upright branches to support themselves rather than having to guide the log's direction.

Progress was slow but it was continuous. Breakneck Hill was long and, at times so steep that the wagon would slide on its locked wheels independent of any pulling by the oxen. Nick Lazoruk's plan was working. When they got to the bend in the trail, the rubble from the previous disaster was still there. Blowflies were not so thick and the odor from dead horses was no longer apparent. Some plants had sprouted amidst the pile of wagon parts and abandoned supplies. Time was obliterating the evidence of broken dreams.

They stopped to rest at the curve, and Fred and Steve walked through the heap lifting a panel here, rolling a can or pail there. They did not take anything; there was nothing they needed, and there was no room to pack more supplies. Their talk was in low tones, as if not to disturb the sanctity of the place.

Erena was gradually approaching the same area. Packing her son on her hip, ducking under branches, or forcing them aside to protect

George's face, grasping for handholds from trunk to trunk, she side-stepped down the incline. Her thoughts, too, were with the pioneers who did not make it. She reached the rubble and tears came to her eyes. These were the remains of a struggle, like hers, probably young and maybe alone — someone's hopes and dreams of a better life dashed near the base of Breakneck Hill.

"How could God," she thought, "permit such wrath upon a man He created?"

Her Orthodox faith, still intact, not having suffered the condemnation her husband and brother had experienced in Vita, Erena saw the new shoots of plant life creeping between the rubble. She felt she had gained an understanding even in tragedy: God's skillful hand would convert this pathetic canvas into a masterpiece of His art. The first strokes of His brush were already visible, and, in time, there would be no sign of the chaos beneath — and life would go on.

Such thoughts were common to the teaching of her Orthodox faith. She could assimilate this catastrophic scene into an understanding of the constancy of life: its cycle, disorder blending with final order, allowing mankind to cope. These thoughts gave her comfort as she wiped the tears from her eyes. She hugged her son tighter, squeezed his face against her own, and proceeded down the hill.

As she rounded the corner she could see that the trail thereafter was flatter. A few stumps were appearing where trees had been cut well above ground level and her husband and her brother had easily maneuvered the oxen around them. A little further on she met Steve, Nick Lazoruk, and Fred returning for the other wagons. Nick Woronuk had stayed with his team on the flat. The men told Erena that they would take all four teams down together, because the log behind kept straight in the rut, and the less disciplined oxen that Fred drove would benefit by the steadiness of the disciplined Chalus team.

Erena reached her husband, and after a brief discussion, left George with him. She turned to climb back to help Maria with her four children negotiate the slope. She met them already part way down, Maria carrying Alyce, and Wasylena trying to guide little two-year-old Steve down the hill. The other two older children, along with their cousin Sadie, found the hill an opportunity to jump from tree to tree, their laughter breaking the silence of the others who needed to concentrate on each step. Old Yakiew was well behind. Every step was chosen with care, his balance compromised and his legs weak; his every step carried with it the risk of a fall, and a disastrous end to his journey. Erena picked up Steve and proceeded down the hill with renewed confidence, having now negotiated it both downward and upward. But Maria, true to her character, holding Alyce in her arms, waited for Domka to help her manage two-year-old Lucy.

Back on top with the wagons, the men tied each cow to the back of the log. They now formed an extended wagon train: the team, the wagon, the breaking pole and a cow. The order of the procession was to allow Chalus to go first because of his stable oxen, behind him Sandul with young oxen needing the Chalus team's security, then Nick Lazoruk, and finally Mike. The men chose to ride the wagons because they would have a more direct control of the reins, but they would work their way into the hay to be able to stand in the box rather than sit on the seat. The slope of the seat during the steepest incline would make it impossible to stay seated without hands to grasp the seat rail. When the descent commenced, the women stopped to observe this terrifying procession. Their concern for the life of their men was expressed by gasps, as wagons slipped sideways, and oxen temporarily lost footing. But they made it! They had Breakneck Hill behind them, and surely, the trail would be better now.

At the bottom of Breakneck, they removed the logs, retied the cattle, and took out the poles that constituted the rough-blocks to the wheels. They had lunch; it was now nearly noon and they had not yet travelled a mile. A drizzle of rain began to fall, and mosquitoes appeared in huge numbers from the grass around them. There was a clear mountain stream, a hundred meters or so up the road, where they got water for cooking and watered the cattle and oxen.

# CHAPTER 19

A great sense of relief overwhelmed them; they had mastered a major obstacle that had frustrated many previous travelers and, unquestionably, would overwhelm some future ones. Even the normally impassive Steve, leaning against the wagon wheel, expressed appreciation for the concept envisaged by Nick Lazoruk that had worked so well.

Fred Sandul was beside himself with the excitement from the descent and could not sit. He paced back and forth, and walked into the bush on the side of the trail where he discovered a cache that included a piano. Obviously, someone was going one way or the other, found this instrument too heavy to transport, and had to discard it. What a pity it seemed; someone's pride, perhaps a talented musician — who knows — lost a valuable instrument in order to gain access to a homestead. Nick Woronuk looked longingly at the piano after Fred pointed out the site to him. A shiver went up his spine; someone may have treasured that piano as he treasured his violin. The issue was weight and size. Personal survival would triumph over pleasure. The piano would remain there, in the tall grass where it may have already been for a year or more.

The rain fell heavier now, and the women covered themselves and the children with the tent canvas as they sat on the hay. It was dark and stuffy in this enclosure, and it wasn't long before the children were screaming as the wagon tipped from side to side over the rough ruts and roots that the wheels could not avoid. There was no alternative; they had to remove the cover and expose the women and children to the elements.

The rain persisted all the rest of the day. Sometimes it was heavy and the children would whimper. The altitude was high enough that the rain felt cold even though it was early September. The women would do what they could to make the children comfortable, but it wasn't possible. Sometimes when the trail was particularly bad and the oxen had to slowly maneuver between the stumps and roots, the women and children would walk behind their wagons. But the road was getting sloppy. It was not mud so much, as pools of water, and walking through them was unavoidable.

The children were wet through and the crying began again. There was no opportunity for the children to run and play, as they would have done normally, and there was no place to dry out. They had to tolerate the weather, and on days such as this, it was exasperating for both mother and child.

Evening approached and they came to the Athabasca River where a small cable ferry took them across, one wagon at a time. They decided to make camp. The oxen were tired, thirsty, and hungry. Still, they calculated, they had traveled a total of 50 miles and had overcome a major obstacle on the trail. Not bad, they agreed. At this rate, in less than two weeks they would be on good pastureland near Sturgeon Lake, the northern end of the Edson Trail. They fed the oxen and the cows well that evening and ate substantially themselves. It was a miscalculation that they would eventually regret.

On the third day, rain continued to fall sporadically. The ground in the deep forest did not absorb the rain; now deep puddles were forming, obscuring the stumps, and making travel slower and rougher. The forest was so thick that the branches above the trail connected across the trail below. The roots that they encountered were often from suckers that had extended from the mother tree. When the wagon wheel struck a stump from such a sucker, it would send vibration though the whole tree, and buckets of water fell onto the wagons. Children screamed, and the mothers wiped them with towels, wet from repeated use, only to have the process recur in the next few moments.

It was remarkable how the children adapted to these conditions. Before the third day was over, they all seemed to tire of crying about conditions that were impossible to control. One by one, they would resort to a whimper and, sometimes, not a sound would emanate from their lips. The parents marveled at the survival instinct of their children. It was understandable how the human race had survived the countless tribulations that faced it in the history of mankind. Maria's children, in particular, were the subjects of evening conversation. Lena, just six years old, would shield the younger two with her own body when they were about to get drenched. Maria had not asked her to protect them; she just seemed to consider it her duty to do so.

Maria did not fuss over Lena's act, expected of someone well beyond her age. She simply pressed Lena against herself, a sign of love and respect. That message seemed more profound than all the superlatives that were directed to her by the other families.

By early afternoon they reached the cabin of the trapper who had offered to keep Nick's and Mike's sheepskin coats. As they approached, no dogs barked, and the door did not open. They knocked but there was no answer. Nick and Mike entered the unlocked cabin; it appeared to have been deserted for some time. They would never learn what had happened to the trapper or to their coats.

The wagon train pushed on for a few more miles, but the persistent rain made travel very uncomfortable. Hoping for better weather the following day, they made camp earlier than on the previous nights. They had travelled 15 miles on their fourth day. In four days they had averaged only 20 miles per day, but if they could maintain that average, they would still get to good pasture before feed ran out.

Nick and Mike discussed the muskeg holes farther up the trail and wondered what condition they would be in if this rain persisted. If the trapper had been around, they could have obtained some information from him. Most travelers on the trail stopped at his cabin, and he likely welcomed them as he did Nick and Mike. The timber remained tall, and so enclosing that they could not be assured of the direction the storm was taking. Their hope was that farther north the weather would be clear. None of the men felt comfortable with hope alone.

It was on their fifth day that they forded a small creek and then found the road worse than they had seen it in the past four days. Nick and Mike were surprised; they remembered this spot. It was where road crews had ceased any upgrading activity. Up to this point, small trees were cut, branches trimmed off, and the trunks laid in a corduroy fashion in bogs. Although rough to ride over, they provided good footing for the oxen and the wagons did not sink into the bog. There were no further signs of camps where working men stayed; it appeared to them that the Government had suddenly lost interest in the Edson Trail. There was still the long shot possibility that farther ahead the camps would be there, but the men were concerned that with the rain and the bog, they would have serious trouble making headway.

In their discussion that evening, they decided that they would limit the feed to the milk cows, to assure there was enough for the oxen. They agreed to begin the rationing in the morning. Steve thought that each person should reduce their food intake to be sure they still had food if the trip took longer than two weeks. There was general agreement on this issue too, and the women agreed to cook a little less each day to allow the adult's bodies to become gradually adjusted to the smaller quantity of food.

No one spoke of it, but each adult knew that they had passed the point of no return on the second day when they overcame the Breakneck Hill obstacle. There was no way the oxen could pull loaded wagons up that hill. They would have to do what the owner of the piano did: drop most of the load and lose their lifelong possessions at the bottom. Returning was thus not an option. They had to go on.

The days passed by. The monotonous repetition of setting up camp each evening, and taking it down in the morning, wore on the women and the men too. The road progressively worsened the farther north they travelled. Low-lying areas were flooded with water, the stumps invisible beneath the murky surface. Each day, it seemed, they were making less progress than the day before. The feed for the cattle had to be seriously curtailed in order to keep the oxen fed.

The milk supply was dropping off precipitously. Their own food supplies were dwindling, and an air of desperation was developing. Domka recognized this, and one evening she set the stage for the rest of the trip. She, despite being pregnant, would eat less and save the food for the children and for the men who toiled so desperately. But the men, too, agreed to do with less to eat. It was clear they would soon be short of food and the animals short of hay.

*My dad and Uncle Mike recalled their trip on foot. They remembered that the forest was dense throughout except for the last few miles before Sturgeon Lake. The sun rarely penetrated the timber, so grass could not grow. What brush there was growing along the trail was not satisfactory for the animals, and they knew that under stress and need, the oxen and the cattle, as Uncle Steve Chalus had said earlier, would eat the brush, but it would not provide energy. Their hope was to find a source of hay they could buy to replenish their supply.*

They were now three weeks into their journey, and the last mile marker that they had seen was 160. They had passed well beyond the halfway mark to Sturgeon Lake and about half way to their destination. The rains had made the road extremely difficult to travel. Over much of this part of the trail, the women and older children walked in order to lessen the load for the starving draft animals. The cows were untied from the wagons and were herded by Yakiew and Wasylena Lazoruk. Yakiew, elderly and tired, never complained, but just moved one foot forward after the other, carrying a walking stick to help maintain balance and probe under the water surfaces for obstacles that could cause him to fall. Had he fallen, it appeared to the others, he would not have been able to raise himself without help. There were still 60 rough miles to go before they reached Sturgeon Lake and from there the road would be better.

One day they met a mail pack train, a man on horseback, and six packhorses in line. They inquired from the mailman if there was any hay along the trail that they could buy. He looked at them, assessed their desperate state, and said there was a supply of hay some fifteen miles farther, but it was not for sale. It was government hay, brought there for his horses so that he had an adequate supply of hay to deliver the mail. He went on to explain that the hay was off to the east a few miles on a wagon trail that was well marked.

It was clear to the men that by telling them where there was hay, even though not for sale, that he recognized their plight, and he opened the door for accessing feed for their animals. They were encouraged by this comment, and then asked him how the trail was farther north. He shook his head and said it was worse than anything they had gone over thus far. "How could it be worse?" Nick asked. "We are making only 10 miles per day now!" The rider pointed to his horses' legs. They were plastered with mud up to their bellies, and his own pants were mud to his thighs. He had seen some rough road, he was tired, but he knew he was over the worst. In his mind he judged that this group would not make it. They were short of all the essentials for survival, and all he could offer was to steal some government hay.

He lingered a bit with them, watching as they crept forward. He looked sadly at old Yakiew with his walking stick picking his way through the muck a foot deep and driving the cattle slowly forward. And Wasylena, younger and stronger, with her head wrapped in white cloth according to her religious tradition, her long skirt dragging in the mud, lifting her boots to make the next step and sometimes pressing on Yakiew's shoulder to add yet another instrument of support to a very tired old man. "Yes," he thought, "some will perish on this road from hell."

The children did not cry anymore. Their faces were gaunt from struggling through mud and bush, and doing so without a sufficient sustaining quality of milk. Erena's Jersey, with her deer-like thin legs, was failing. She would fall and Yakiew and Wasylena would urge her up; she would stumble forward a few more paces, stop with her front legs wide apart, and lower her head nearly to the mud. Yakiew would bring her water and a handful of hay, but she would refuse to eat and drink. She was dying.

Many times the women recalled the curse that the pastor had levied upon Nick Woronuk and Mike. Was it possible that these hardships were the consequence of not paying their dues to the church? The power of such incantation was foremost in the minds of Wasylena and

Elana Chalus. As they walked, they prayed for salvation, for the Lord's help to crush the pastor's curse. The two men listened to the women's lamentations, and reminded them that in the same breath, the pastor had blessed both Nick Lazoruk and Steve, who had paid their dues, and yet they were suffering equally. Even the youthful and endlessly energetic Fred Sandul had lost his enthusiasm, and had become impassive.

Whether spurred by the mailman's words of available hay, or by his inherent optimism that had carried him through the trauma of leaving his mother in Onut, or convincing the group to venture into the Peace River Country, or struggling with the English language, Nick Woronuk remained positive in his purpose. His personality and his vivaciousness helped overcome the developing depression that was progressively subduing others in the group. He felt that depression had the potential to kill even more than the lack of food. He would do what was necessary to ease their concerns, just as he had by endlessly teasing his sisters in Onut, to ease the burden of his departure on his mother. In his tent in the evening, he bounced little George on his knee and whistled lively tunes to make the boy laugh and giggle. George was no longer able to walk and Erena was extremely worried by the weakness of her son. As much as they urged him and stood him on his feet, he would collapse and crawl even though now nearly fourteen months old.

Steve Chalus continued to be a paradox. During travel, he maintained a constant scream at his oxen, often relentlessly whipping them regardless of the conditions through which they traveled. Yet, in the evening, when all the others were resting, this powerful man would gently currycomb the animals, scraping off the mud from their flanks, showing an appreciation in direct contrast to his attitude during the work day. He seemed indifferent to the pangs of pain that he must have suffered along with all the adults, and to some degree, the children too.

Rest was no more than an interruption in the day's obligations. So it would be throughout his life.

# CHAPTER 20

T he mailman resumed his travel southward as the wagon train disappeared into the woods northward. The sight he had seen weighed on him. When he finally reached Edson, he told the blacksmith about what he had seen, and that he suspected that, at best, only some of the group would survive the trip. On a later return to Edson, the men in the group learned of this prediction and felt that an invisible Hand had played a part in proving him wrong.

But such proof was not without serious tests. Potholes in the trail were common, and there was always the risk of what was invisible below the surface. On one such occasion, Erena was sitting next to Nick on the wagon seat holding her son with both hands. The oxen, their noses close to the muddy surface, seemed to be sniffing for a proper pathway as they slowly lumbered on through the hole. Suddenly there was a loud thump and the wagon jerked upward and to the right throwing Nick, Erena and George off their seat and into the sludge. The impact was so sudden and violent that George flew out of his mother's arms, and splashed into the mud inches from the left front wheel. Erena screamed; Nick shouted at the oxen to stop. The animals, obedient to the command, stopped instantly. The left wheel of the wagon was resting on the stump it had hit, the wagon skewed to the right, and the child lay screaming in the mud directly against the front of the stump. An inch or two more, and the wagon wheel would have crushed his life from him.

Erena clamored over the oxen's traces, somehow managed to climb over the center pole, and fell to her knees to retrieve her son. The rest of the travelers heard her screams and rushed to help. Amidst cries of anguish, and praise to God, they calmed the distraught mother and the crying child she clutched to her breast.

For the remainder of the voyage to Sturgeon Lake, neither Erena nor any of the other women would sit on the driver's seat again. The men moved articles around in their wagon boxes to provide room for the women and children. Erena was too frightened to accept this compromise; she chose to walk and carry her son for miles, until she could no longer continue. Reluctantly, she took the place that Nick had provided for her in their wagon.

*Mother tried to add to conversation that evening around the table, regarding this frightening experience, but tears welled in her eyes and her voice choked. She turned from the table and sobbed again, and the women wept with her. It was a while before conversation resumed. That tragic event affected all present, including me. Seeing my mother sobbing, and tears in my dad's eyes, made me cry too. Mother noticed. She came to me, hugged me against her waist, and wiped my eyes with her apron. It was damp, I remember, from her tears.*

The following day they reached the first mud-hole that the mailman had described. It was long, perhaps 100 meters, with no visible objects above its waterline. The land to the west sloped upwards, and the women and children left the wagons to wend their way through the timber on higher ground to rejoin the road at the end of this quagmire.

It had turned cold and occasional flurries of sleet and snow began to fall. The ground beneath their feet was soft and spongy. It was muskeg, a seemingly bottomless muck that they had encountered at the beginning of their trip. Previously the road crew had laid a corduroy of cut timber to make passage possible. No such advantage here. The men stopped to survey the obstacle ahead of them. Nick Woronuk and Steve Chalus, the two still showing stamina, decided to walk the length with poles to check the depth of mud and the firmness of the invisible base over which they must travel.

It took an hour before they returned. Their poles indicated that the ground level was about a foot below the surface but it was soft and they had sunk another several inches into the muskeg with each step. It was frightening; it seemed bottomless. They were afraid to stand in one spot for fear of sinking too deep to extricate their feet. How would the oxen manage? Their weight would push them deeper into the muck. And then there were the wagon wheels; how deep would they sink, and could the oxen pull the load? Of all the obstacles they had faced, this might well be the most formidable.

Steve and Nick discussed each aspect and decided that Nick would take his load across first as a test. After all, the mailman had made it across with all his horses, and horses were not as compliant as oxen, Nick reasoned. Chalus agreed. If he were in charge of the first crossing, he would drive them through ruthlessly, as was his habit to do. But that was not Nick's nature. He would let the oxen set their own pace. They had traversed countless mud puddles in the past days and weeks and were well accustomed to the ordeals that existed below the surface water.

When they returned, soaked above their knees, the other men had gone farther back. Erena's cow had fallen again and their prodding and lifting could not raise her. With help from Nick and Steve, they

151

were able to get her off the trail, and they agreed that it would be impossible for her to go on. She would have to be left there to die.

Nick's throat tightened and tears welled in his eyes. He knew how Erena would react: she would be devastated. The value of a cow to their child's survival was vital. Starvation had caused each family's cow to reduce its milk production to scarcely serve the needs of the children of that one family. The dying jersey only produced a few cups per day, but even that was better than none at all. How would George, already unable to walk, manage without that nutrition? For however Nick felt, Erena would feel much worse. There was still the bog ahead to attempt. *There may be much more sorrow before this day is over,* Nick remembered thinking.

Dripping wet, he climbed onto his seat on the wagon and turned his oxen into the muskeg. Their first few steps confirmed that there could be serious trouble ahead. They labored to extricate each cloven hoof from the mud below. Even before the hind wheels of the wagon were in the bog, they were straining against the load behind them. The wagon sank; the front end of the wagon box was now below the water level and threatening to float it from its pegs on the frame. As the team pulled the wagon, its load increased from mud that had built up on its front.

Steve only looked for a moment; his mind made up, he returned to his team and began to unhitch them from his wagon.

Nick had gone less than ten meters. His team halted and could pull no more. Standing there motionless, their legs sank to where their bellies were touching the water. The animals stood there staring ahead dumbly and puffing from their exertion. Unlike most horses, they did not panic — just stood there — slowly sinking deeper; waiting for their master to invent some system to save them.

Nick and Mike Lazoruk and Fred Sandul stood at the edge discussing the pitiful sight. Steve Chalus drove his team into the muskeg with his usual screams, his whip cracking the air like rifle shots. His team did not hesitate to enter the quagmire. They pushed their way by the halted wagon and the Woronuk team. The whip cracked behind their necks: they knew that signal meant to back up. The yoke that Chalus had built fit so that the animal's horns prevented the harness from sliding off over the animal's heads. They backed into position in front of the Woronuk team.

Chalus clove hitched the ropes he dragged to the pole of the Woronuk wagon, jerked it tight behind a pin to prevent it from slipping forward, stepped to the side and signaled Nick to prod his team. Four oxen, pulling with all their strength, the wagon moved forward. They would move some 50 yards and rest — but not long: Chalus was in front, and in charge. He would dictate the terms of rest, and rest was a meaningless term to him. Catch their breath, yes, rest — no! But they made it across. Without a word, he unhitched his team and drove it back to hitch onto the Nick Lazoruk wagon. Meanwhile, Nick Woronuk watered and fed his team some of the remaining bits of hay. He unhitched them and waited for the Chalus-Lazoruk combination to make it through. Woronuk and Chalus took turns double-teaming the oxen to bring along the remaining wagons. As the last wagon was brought in, the lead oxen were fatigued and took more rests. The day turned to evening; there was no strength left to go on. They made camp.

Erena did not yet know that her milk cow had to be abandoned to die on the side of the road, just miles from where hay was stored. When Yakiew brought up the cattle, Erena immediately saw that her jersey was absent. She suspected the problem but tearfully asked anyway. Nick told her, and she burst into sobs. To her this cow was no ordinary animal; it represented the best possible source of nutrition for her son, perhaps even the source of saving him from starvation, if the remaining cattle should perish. But the remarkable Maria at once offered a solution. She had ample breast milk for Alyce; she would be a wet nurse for George.

Sometime, somewhere, this gracious woman will be rewarded. Her inherent kindness even in dreadful times like these overwhelmed those around her.

Mike Lazoruk was beginning to show the cardinal signs of severe fatigue from exertion and lack of nutrition. In the depth of the forest, game was rare, for it too had little to forage on. The occasional rabbit would appear and Nick Woronuk would quickly draw a bead on it. They would share the animal for dinner. Sometimes a grouse would fly up. Nick would stop the oxen and carefully view its course until it settled on a log or in a tree that camouflaged it in dry branches. Nick had become expert at anticipating where it would land and it would provide morsels of meat for the group.

The potatoes they had dug were separated into two groups: one for consumption and one for seed. The consumption pile was all but gone, and they had, for days, carefully apportioned the few remaining until they could get to Sturgeon Lake and the Hudson's Bay Store situated there. The carrots, beets, onions and garlic were gone. They were, by definition, starving.

The seed potatoes could suffice to keep them going for no longer than a day or two and then there would be no more. But the seed potatoes also offered a guarantee for survival in the future. They could not be used for food except if circumstances got so desperate that no alternative was possible. It depended on the condition of the road ahead.

So near and yet so far; they considered stopping their travel and have two men walk for food to the Hudson Bay store, somewhere near

Sturgeon Lake. The plan had a failing, however. Holding their spot for any length of time would spell disaster to the animals. There was no feed left. The oxen were foraging on the willows on the side of the road, a food for which their metabolism was not suited. Though it filled a portion of their ruminant stomach, it did not regurgitate well and they would vomit rather than chew their cud.

The Woronuk and Chalus animals still seemed able to work, but the other younger and weaker oxen would tire easily. They would stop without a command to do so, and simply stand there — motionless. They did not seem to be short of breath, they did not puff, they would just hang their heads lower than usual and stand for a minute or two and then, as if by a signal to continue, they would begin to move forward again. Nick Lazoruk knew this sign to mean they were weak from starvation. They would not last much longer.

They awoke in the morning to a foot of snow— and it was continuing to fall. It was the first major snowfall of the year, and it was wet and heavy. Spruce and pine branches were arched downward from the weight, resembling snow ghosts. The scene might have been beautiful under other circumstances, but with the condition of this wagon train, it was depressing and frightening.

According to the mailman, there was yet another muskeg hole to cross before reaching the supply of hay. The distance was about ten miles but with the weakened animals, it would take two days. That morning Steve Chalus had hitched up first. Whether by design or by coincidence, he took the lead. As usual, he was merciless to his oxen and drove them with his routine shouts and whip. Remarkably, the train, with tired and starved animals, somehow followed. The pace Chalus set was high, and he would allow the animals rest time only while crossing streams in order to drink.

The women rode in the wagon boxes, but the roots and stumps they drove over vibrated the trees causing them to shed their snow, blanketing everyone. Children screamed, mothers consoled, but the drivers scarcely looked back, trying to wend their way between stumps. Chalus had set an unrelenting pace. It was a chaotic day, but they were covering ground.

By early afternoon they arrived at the next major bog — one the mailman had described as the worst. When they unhitched and began to make camp, Steve again first curried his animals and showed a gentle side that was totally absent during the day.

*In later days, discussing this trip over coffee, the men agreed that this "forced march" might have saved the expedition. Yes, Chalus was merciless, but some of the oxen may have died had another day been needed to reach the hay.*

The last bog was about the same length as the one before. Again, Woronuk and Chalus waded through to test the depth and conditions under the surface. Part way through, they found one hole that reached about four feet in depth, and even deeper adding the soft bottom. This was a major obstacle; they knew that their animals, harnessed to the wagons, would not survive in that depth. It was likely the hole that muddied the mailman's horses up to their bellies. The rest of the bog was difficult but not worse than the one they had crossed a day earlier. This hole had to be repaired before they could attempt the crossing. They would have to cut timber and lay it across the depression as the road builders had done. Corduroying this one spot would allow the oxen to cross without plunging them to the bottom — possibly drowning them.

Each man took an axe and felled the smaller pine, trimmed off their branches and dragged them over the hole in the road. Five experienced woodsmen, though tired and weakened by hunger, soon had sufficient logs to bridge the hole. The remaining problem was to sink them and pile enough of them, one on top of the other, to hold the weight of a team. The area was rocky and they rolled a few rocks onto the ends of the logs and they gradually sank. Now all that was left was to try to cross.

In the morning, they walked across the bridge several times and found it stable underfoot. Oxen, however, detest uncertain footing. Optimally, the logs should have been spiked one to the other to prevent them from slipping and spooking the oxen, but no one carried spikes.

To negotiate this hole they hitched three teams together. To lead, they used Woronuk's team, then Nick Lazoruk's, and hitched to the wagon was the Chalus team. Slowly the six oxen drew the Chalus wagon to the bridge they had built. The Woronuk team placed their front legs on the logs and instantly stopped. Nick Lazoruk, leading them and speaking gently, stepped onto the logs to show their stability. Steve Chalus, holding the reins on his team, remained silent. Nick's gentle manner helped; the animals, their eyes wide with fright, pushed themselves onto the bridge. Their weight may have pushed the bridge logs deeper into the bog and helped stabilize them from rolling underfoot. As the Woronuk team led the way, the other oxen followed.

The women had found a way around the bog through snow, carrying, leading, and urging the children with them. They were on the north end of the muskeg patch, waiting and anxiously watching their men manage this hazardous procedure. They knew full well that if the first wagon did not make it across, none of the others would.

There was no time to waste. The snow was melting, the water was getting deeper and the chance for success with the other wagons was becoming more doubtful by the hour. They unhitched and drove the oxen back into the muskeg to return for the next wagon. By early evening, they had crossed the last obstacle that surely would have defeated most other wagon trains that season. They harnessed the teams to their wagons and proceeded up the trail to a stream where they could get water and make camp. That day they had travelled only a single mile.

# CHAPTER 21

Y ou remember, Mike, when you were so tired you could not continue," Steve recalled. "We were worried that you might not make it alive."

Again — silence. Maybe time was needed to gather a recall of that frightening time, or perhaps it was just that the occasion was so tragic that words would not come. Mike, trying to make light of the occasion, finally broke the silence. "It might be that I was just lazy. I knew if I pretended to be so hungry, someone might bring me a roast."

But Nick, his brother interrupted. "Your color, Mike, was the color of death. You changed so rapidly. I couldn't believe what I was seeing; you were changing from a living person to one no longer alive, all in a matter of part of an hour. You owe your life to Nick and his scrounging skills."

*Uncle Nick Lazoruk's description obviously must have struck a note with all present. There was silence again as each man's mind went back to that time, years ago, when Mike's life seemed to be hanging in a balance and depended on the availability of food. The subject was quickly dismissed, almost as though it was an*

*embarrassment. But for me, it lingered, and sometime later I asked my dad for an*
*explanation. He explained it this way:*

"Starvation had a different effect on Mike Lazoruk than it did on the other members of the group. He was hardy, but he was lighter, and his energy reserve seemed less. He needed food sooner and more critically than the rest of us. Sitting by his tent stove, drying out his clothes, his color suddenly turned grey, and he was not able to stand up. Domka came to our tent and told me to come see for myself.

"I immediately walked over and could see that Mike, my best friend, was in a desperate condition and that food was critical. His speech was slurred and he felt cold and clammy. He may have been going into shock, and if that direction was not reversed, he could lose his life. Clinical signs of hunger were unknown to me, but I recognized the strange appearance of my friend and his lack of normal responsiveness. I advised Domka to keep the tent warmer than usual, and I would go in search of food. What I had in mind was to hunt the area around our camp, and if I could not find anything, I was going to try to find the Hudson's Bay Store some ten miles away.

"I told Erena of her brother's state, picked up my .22 caliber rifle, and with dusk setting in, began a search for whatever I could shoot that would provide meat for a dying man. On one circle about our camp, I found a garbage dump that others had used in earlier travels. I kicked through the refuse and found a pail laying on its side with something in it. Turning it up I was stunned to find a whole half pork rib cage. It had been there for some time, and during the warmer weather, blow-flies had laid their eggs. The meat smelled badly, and the underside was covered with maggots.

"I did not hesitate. I took pail and meat, maggots and all, directly to the stream but a few steps away. Using the pail I threw buckets of water across the meat, then scrubbed the surface with my hands. In the twilight, I could no longer see maggots flipping from side to side. Making sure the pail was clean, I filled it with water and hauled the meat and water to the tent.

"Domka had stoked the fire well. Most of the adults had come in to attempt to raise Mike's spirits, but when I arrived, he seemed only partly aware of my presence.

"Meat," I shouted, "enough meat for you, Metro, and some for the rest of us too. Wake up, my friend, we are going to have a feast."

Mike smiled faintly at his good friend but still was not aware of what the special occasion was about. Domka, meanwhile, had the bucket on the stove heating the water and the meat that Nick had brought. She did not mention to anyone what she was picking from the surface from time to time. They were maggots that Nick had not discovered.

When the water was getting warm, more maggots appeared, and the other women noticed Domka frequently skimming the surface with a ladle and throwing the contents out the tent opening. She added the last of her potatoes, and with that, Erena, Elana, Maria, and Wasylena all left to get what vegetables they had to add to the meat. Tonight was going to be a communal dinner, a feast indeed — but perhaps their last.

There was far more meat than an ideal stew would require, but it was meat they felt that Mike needed, and that they all craved. The fat from the ribs floated to the surface, the boiling water under it causing it to splatter onto the hot stove surface. Smoke filled the tent: smoke with the aroma of sizzling fat that the group had not smelled for weeks. No one questioned the quality of the meat Nick had found. All waited for their portion.

It was a late supper. Domka chose to overdo the meat by taking it out of the stew and frying it in a pan before serving it. The meat fell off the ribs, and with the stew, was indeed the finest meal they had eaten in a long time.

Mike ate a little, and though he seemed at first to be unable to eat a substantial amount, his appetite soon returned, and he ate a hearty meal. His color rapidly improved, and everyone felt relieved when he said it was too warm in the tent. For Mike, that meal might have saved his life. The entire group, including the older children, felt their energy return and began to play and run, activity that had been lost to them for nearly a month.

Maria breastfed Alyce on one breast and held George to feed from the other. Without this wonderful woman, George may not have survived, or if he had, he may have suffered in his development. Erena reminded Maria how blessed George was to have such an aunt, and that she would teach him to respect Maria throughout his life. And she did this, not with George alone, but with all the children she would have in the future. To the Woronuk family, Aunt Maria was like a second mother.

By morning Mike had regained some strength. The other men hitched his oxen to his wagon and provided a little assistance for him to climb to his seat. All were anxious to reach the hay, a mere six miles on a road that was now significantly better. Even in their weakened state, the oxen could pull the near empty wagons that distance.

They set out early in the morning to reach the point the mailman had said that hay was stored. But before noon another problem arose. A rider on horseback caught up to them and asked whose cow that was back several miles. Nick told him it was his and that she was unable to go any further. The rider understood that, but he told Nick he would have to return and kill her. He could not leave her there suffering. In fact, he said, Nick could be fined for allowing the animal to suffer so.

The rider never did identify himself. Whether he was an officer of the law or not, he did seem to carry an air of authority.

Nick had considered shooting Jenny when the decision was made to leave her behind. However, he had not been able to bring himself to do it. She had been invaluable to his son's survival; she would come to the family to be petted, milked, or fed whenever called. His attachment to this animal was second only to Erena's. To Erena, this was the first animal she could claim as her own. She had raised her from a calf on the Lazoruk farm in Arbakka. The two were so attached to each other that at the instant Jenny would spot her, she would raise her head from grazing, or rise up from lying down, and run to her. Erena would caress her behind the ears and neck, and Jenny would rub the side of her head against Erena's hip and arm. It developed into a remarkable human-animal relationship.

Nick picked up his .22 rifle and shells and set a fast pace to return to the cow. After two hours he found her where they had left her. She looked at him and clearly recognized him. But tears flowed down her face; she seemed to sense the reason for his return. Nick choked, his throat tightened, and tears flowed down his face as well. He was so distraught that he would have been unable to see the sights on his gun so he came right up to her. He placed the barrel of the gun against her forehead, and between gasps, he pulled the trigger.

Nick did not wait. He turned, sick from grief, anxious to leave the area — as though it were a crime scene. Gasping, his eyes burning, he made his way back to the group.

Erena had been weeping all the time Nick was gone. Though she knew that the cow's suffering had now ended, she still held on to a desperate fantasy that something miraculous would happen: that perhaps Jenny had survived, and Erena would see Nick leading her to the group, and she would have her animal back. Now this last hope was dashed when she saw her husband approaching, eyes red from his sorrow. She burst into sobs. Nick held her while the other men hitched up his oxen. They climbed aboard without further talk, and resumed their travel to the hay that might have saved Jenny, had she had the strength to proceed for just one more day.

*Mother never did get over the loss of Jenny, her pet and provider. Her appreciation for the value of a cow as an integral life-providing animal never changed. Over a half century after losing Jenny, she still was unable to discuss the event without tears streaming down her cheeks, and her voice would hesitate from that memory.*

By evening they found a wagon trail that veered off to the right, and to the left was an area where others on the trail had camped. They stopped their oxen and made camp. The women began to settle the children and to invent something for the group to eat. There was still broth from the night before, but little more. They knew that if there were hay, the oxen would make Sturgeon Lake the following day. If there was no feed, it would be two days or more, or perhaps the animals would not survive at all. As soon as they got off their wagons, Nick Woronuk and Nick Lazoruk followed the trail to the right in search of the haystack.

Having walked a mile or two, it was getting dark, and just as they were preparing to return, assuming this to be the wrong trail, there it was: a substantial haystack, properly compressed, and covered from the weather with sheets of tarpaulin. There wasn't another person around. The stack was set back from the main trail, enough to be easily missed by poachers such as themselves. They gathered as much hay as they could carry on their backs and began the trek back.

It was dark when they returned. Mike Lazoruk had regained more strength and was able to help Steve Chalus and Fred Sandul set up the four tents. They had already eaten and were waiting for the two Nicks to return. They divided the hay between the five teams, and the two men went in to eat, and to describe their find. They decided to empty two wagons and bring all the teams to the stack, where the oxen could feed and the men could pilfer enough for a few more days. In the short time it took to reassemble, the oxen had eaten the little hay apportioned to each one and were turning and twisting their heads for more. The Woronuk and Sandul teams were hitched to their wagons for the return trip, now in darkness.

The plan was a good one. The Government of Alberta had graciously, although unknowingly, saved this group of settlers from the potential of having lost some, if not all, of their draft animals. Kind words were repeated about the generous information that the mailman had offered. The eventual agricultural success of these early settlers repaid the Province of Alberta countless times by their produce and taxes.

# CHAPTER 22

Nick Woronuk was fatigued. He had rushed nearly ten miles to where they had left Jenny, suffered from having to destroy her, and then rushed back. He walked in to find the hay, packed all he could manage to the camp, retraced his walk with oxen, helped stack a three or four day supply, and returned to the camp. Such exertion would have taxed a fit man, but Nick was starving. It was his dogged determination, very much a component of his character, that drove him that day, and it was that same characteristic that helped ensure a final successful farming settlement for all four families. It was well into the morning hours when he finally got to bed, still underfed, feeling some anxiety for having stolen for the first time in his life, and it left him unable to sleep or rest well.

He found himself unsteady on his feet when he arose in the morning, much as Mike Lazoruk had experienced when he had been overcome by fatigue. Nick knew his responsibility to the group: he had initiated it, had guided it most of the way, and now near to claiming success, he was in danger of failing them. Erena could see his unsteadiness and hear his slightly slurred speech, and she became concerned. She spoke of her worry to her father, Yakiew. He, too, had noticed that his son-in-law was at the end of his endurance. Now that the oxen had good feed, they could tie the milk cows again to the back of the wagons, and he and Wasylena could ride. They boarded the Woronuk wagon and Yakiew drove.

Old and frail, Yakiew took the reins from Nick and directed him to the hay in his box to rest. No one thought that this elderly man would last more than an hour or two. Unlike horses, these oxen were not trained to take a bit in the mouth. Their reins were tied to a halter, then passed through a ring in the yoke. It took a great deal of force to signal the team to turn when they were not responding sufficiently to the verbal commands. Most turning was by voice command: a "gee" (to the right) or a "haw" (to the left) depending on the direction they needed to turn. The road, although much better than they had seen in many days, still had stumps to maneuver around, and that fine tuning needed rein guidance. Yakiew, as an old veteran of driving oxen, performed remarkably. It was well into the afternoon before he allowed his son-in-law to take over again. His help had been indispensible. Nick Woronuk would have had a difficult time, or may not have succeeded at all, were it not for this tenacious and kind man.

Rather quickly, the forest changed from dense evergreen trees of spruce and pine to a combination favoring leafless aspen poplar. They were coming out of the mountains, and little patches of clear prairie appeared with the tips of grass penetrating a thinning blanket of snow. It was feed for the cattle and oxen. Now they felt assured they would make it!

They pressed ahead; the Woronuk and Chalus oxen remained stronger, perhaps stimulated by the scent from occasional tufts of grass on the sides of the trail. The other three teams were struggling despite the minimal load they were pulling. The wagon train was approaching Sturgeon Lake, and the group was depending on the local natives and the Hudson's Bay Store to replenish their food supply.

Each mile the dense growth of spruce and pine diminished, and poplar grew randomly in patches within progressively larger meadows. Snow had melted from the knolls, and green and brown fall grass was showing. A native settlement was to the right a few hundred yards and a meadow to the left. Ponies, with improvised hobbles and tiny bells hanging around their necks, raised their heads and ambled closer to the trail for a better view. The sun broke through cumulous clouds and rivulets from snowmelt crisscrossed the trail. Native peoples, domesticated animals, sunlight and meadows; it was like an epiphany, a sudden realization that twentieth century man cannot live alone. This was a welcome return to civilization.

They decided to make camp there. They knew the animals would feed well on the grass, and the men could get food from the natives or directions to the Hudson's Bay Store. Nick and Mike went to the settlement; the others were preparing to take the oxen to a stream for water before letting them feed in the meadow.

There was an ominous strangeness in the air as the two men approached the settlement. No one acknowledged their presence with other than a glare. When they approached one native man sitting beside his teepee and asked for food for children in exchange for money, he grunted, irritably, "No food, no money, go to store."

They were stunned. In all their travels they had encountered only the kindest people, willing to help the settler however possible. This was a clear exception. Stories had radiated around, as stories do, about the hostility of the Indians, but they had not encountered it before.

They learned later that these were nomadic hunter-gatherers, not fishermen. Settlers, like Nick and Mike, were inhabiting their traditional native territory, their leader, Louis Riel, had been hanged, and their future was uncertain. White man was responsible. Their disposition was understandable.

Nick and Steve made a hasty retreat to their camp and returned before the tents were unloaded. They explained their reception and decided to move away from the perceived danger that such proximity to the native camp presented. They re-hitched the oxen and moved toward Sturgeon Lake.

Now the terrain was changing to a gently rolling plain. Large plots of land were free of any growth other than scrub brush and willow. "This," explained Nick to Erena, "is a little like the land we have as homesteads."

"So much land is free of trees," she exclaimed. "Room for pasture and one can even plow a few areas without any trees to remove. I can have a garden in the spring," she added, and for the first time in weeks, her voice carried its characteristic lilt. She pressed George closer to herself and her dreams began to revive.

"Maybe, maybe," she said softly, "this might all be worth it."

They were now entering the touted Peace River Country, where a railway would soon be built, grain grew tall with the long summer days, and gardens were lush, like she remembered in Bukovina. It would take time, she knew, but one day they would prosper, and life would be easier for George and other children she would have.

They were around 100 miles from home! In the next week they might unload the wagons for the last time; they would have to live in the tent — but anything would be better than the last two months. Erena imagined a stable household of her own, living as neighbors to her relatives. They could visit back and forth as often as they wished, and the children would play together, and it would be home.

Her mind raced from one thought to another. The hardships she had endured somehow made the hopes she had for the future even brighter. She vowed to herself, in the privacy of her heart, that she would help Maria, that saint of a woman, to raise her family and provide for them. She would be like a second mother to the Nick Lazoruk children, just as Maria had become to her son.

There was a clearing with no native settlements in view, a lush pasture of grass protruded through the snow, and a little stream ran clear water from melting snow just a few paces ahead. This was an ideal spot to make camp. Sturgeon Lake could be seen through the sparse timber a short distance away.

Nick Woronuk and Steve unhitched their teams and let the oxen out to pasture. Almost immediately, the animals pawed the thin layer of snow away to expose the full blades of succulent grass. Throwing their heads up from time to time seemed to be an expression of their joy at feasting. The animals were thriving, but the humans were still starving. As the other wagons were approaching, Steve and Nick walked to the lake in search of a native fishing settlement to buy fish.

From the lakeshore they could see several native encampments near the water's edge. They approached the first of these and found the natives communicative. Several men gathered around the two white travelers to listen to their requests. They had fish, fresh or dried, but they wanted to trade, and as best Steve and Nick could understand, it was to trade for liquor. Neither Steve nor Nick carried any, but with hand motions and shaking heads they were able to get their messages across. Nick showed them paper money but the native men were still indecisive.

Steve Chalus reached deep into his pocket and retrieved some Canadian coins. The shiny silver ones were of immediate interest and a bargain was made. They took what coins Steve had and brought out more fish than the two men could pack. One of the young native men brought a hand-spun blanket, loaded the fish into it, tied its corners securely and threw it over his back with such ease that the load appeared weightless. As they began to walk back, someone brought another four fish that were somewhat different in color and shape. The men found out later that these were pickerel, a favorite among the natives and whites.

It was later learned that the coins the natives took would never be used for money; they would be drilled and strung on leather bands to form decorative necklaces, just as their own wives wore when dressed in Ukrainian attire. The world somehow seemed smaller then. There really were no differences between natives and whites. All are humans.

The young native set a fast pace. He was tall and raw-boned with jet-black hair beyond his shoulders, and his strength was remarkable. He carried perhaps seventy pounds of fish, while Steve and Nick each carried two small pickerel; they were soon winded, whereas he showed no fatigue at all.

He suddenly turned right on a narrow footpath that led southward through thick willow and alder. They followed him, a little reluctantly, not sure where this path would lead. To their astonishment, it exited within a short distance of their camp. The natives knew their exact location all along, and the idea that they had distanced themselves from the first group was unfounded.

*Years later, sitting around the table that evening, while recalling this incident, they realized that the unfriendly natives had a complete knowledge of the activities in the countryside, without needing addresses such as streets and avenues. They undoubtedly knew where the new camp was made, and the concern that the group had for its safety was not justified.*

The tall, high cheeked, long haired, brown skinned native walked, without the slightest hesitation, into the midst of women and children.

The children rushed to their mothers and hid in their skirts. The men had set up tents, and then had walked into the pasture to see to it that their animals had found water, leaving Yakiew with the women and children in camp. Nick and Steve were still a substantial distance behind. Most of the women and children were frightened, but Domka stood squarely facing him, her feet well apart, and her hands on her hips; her ample abdomen protruding. She stared at him with suspicion but showed no fear. Without changing his facial expression, he slipped the bag to the ground, jerked it to unload the fish onto the grass, turned, and walked away.

He met Steve and Nick returning on the trail, but he stared straight ahead as they passed. He had not waited for any expression of gratitude for packing the fish, nor was there a smile or any recognition of the two men he met. He understood his commitment, fulfilled it, and credits of any kind were redundant. They would never see him again, but they would learn from experiences with other natives that few spoken words were ever needed. In their culture, recognition of good deeds did not depend on verbal expression.

The Lazoruk and Sandul teams were exhausted. The oxen would feed for half an hour or so and lie down to rest, rise a few minutes later, eat and rest again. The men realized that it would take some time for the animals to regain their health and strength. Although the load they pulled now was comparatively light, the weeks of starvation were slowing their recovery.

The men, their spirits much improved after a substantial meal of fried and smoked fish, made plans for the rest of the trip. Chalus was anxious to locate land since no application had been made in his name, and he wanted land near the others. They agreed that the three wagons with the weaker oxen would stay and allow them to feed until they regained their strength; the Chalus and Woronuk wagons would go on to the Spirit River settlement.

That night they slept well. With their stomachs full of the fat and protein that the fish provided, tea from clean stream water, and a smattering of seed potatoes that they decided to use, they were better fed than they had been for weeks. The night was cold and frosty, and the men needed to stoke the camp stoves to keep the children warm. The morning was refreshing, with bright sunlight and a cloudless sky. The group talked about not seeing the sky, veiled for so long by dense timber on the trail, and how much they had missed its brightness, along with the ability to forecast the weather that day.

The terrain around Sturgeon Lake was slightly rolling, and some areas had been hand cleared of trees and bushes, and then sown to hay. It had yielded well. There was great hope for the future.

The obtrusive native they had first met had waved his hand to the east when he mentioned the "store." Nick and Steve chose to walk that direction and bring back food supplies, particularly vegetables, enough to last the rest of the trip to Grande Prairie. After a few miles, close to the water, they saw a two-storey building, sheeted on the outside with rough sawn lumber and with a Hudson's Bay Company sign spiked to the wall above the door. The men walked in.

The smell of tanned hides was overwhelming. The room had hides of every animal in the area in various stages of drying, and other hides in bales taking up half the floor space. The shelves, few that there were, held boxes of shells of several calibers. What space remained was stocked with traps, rifles, snare wire, chain, and rope. Where were the groceries?

A little man smoking a large pipe appeared from behind one of the bales of hides. He greeted the men with a loud "'*ello.*" He was French or French-Canadian and his English was just sufficient to serve the normal clientele that came to the store. Nick asked if he could buy groceries. The storekeeper answered that he did not carry any. His business only supplied the Indians with their needs. They ate fish, not groceries. He did not carry a single item that Nick and Steve needed. The trip was in vain. They would have to survive on fish until they reached Grande Prairie.

By early afternoon the two men returned to camp. There was exquisite alder-smoked fish, left over from what the women had prepared, and Nick and Steve ate. They rounded up their oxen, and hitched them to the wagons to set out for the Smoky River. Three wagons would remain at this site until their oxen had recovered. It was mid-afternoon when the Woronuk and Chalus wagons started out, following a much-improved trail westward.

# CHAPTER 23

hen Nick stopped to make camp, Steve insisted that they
travel on to the river. His shouts at his oxen were constant, and it affected Nick's team as well. They raised their head and, at times, even trotted for short distances. It was dark and cold when they reached the Smoky River, and the animals had to be fed and watered before camp was made. Erena and Elana dragged out the tent canvasses and tried to assemble the poles in the dark, while the children remained sleeping in their wagons. Elana's cow was milked and she shared the milk with Erena. Maria, of course, had stayed back with her husband and now would not be able to breastfeed George.

The following morning they woke to grinding noises coming from the river. It was ice; some chunks several feet in diameter were floating down the river, colliding with each other, producing a sound that resembled steel grinding on steel. The noise was ominous.

The two families assessed this situation and wondered about crossing with a cable ferry that would surely build up with ice. The cable could be overloaded to where it might snap and free the ferry to float, out of control, downstream.

The ferryman was not anxious to allow the wagons to load but, with some persuasion, he motioned for them to drive their rigs on. The bank to the water's edge was steep but Steve did not hesitate. He yelled at the oxen and they obeyed him from habit and slipped and slid down the short but treacherous ten feet to the ferry ramp.

Nick Woronuk's team followed, and the ferryman raised the ramp and cranked the cable to turn the nose into the current. Slowly the force of the water against the side of the ferry forced it to creep away from the shore. The ice was building up on the upstream side of the ferry causing a tendency to over-rotate, then it would slip away and the ferry would momentarily lose its forward motion. All movement seemed to be in slow motion as the ferryman cranked to restore the angle, then cranked the opposite way to prevent the ferry from over-rotating. He directed the men to take long poles to keep as much ice from the ferry as they could. With their help and the operator's skill, they reached a location some two wagon lengths from shore. There the ferry hung up on a shoal, and with the heavy load, could move no further.

There was only one option: drive the oxen with the wagons into the water, at this point around three feet deep. The ferryman dropped the apron and Steve Chalus, with whip and shouts, forced his oxen to suddenly leap forward into the river. The sudden jcrk caused the pole of the wagon to come free of the yoke ring in which it rested. When the wagon struck the water, the pole tip dipped downwards and became anchored in the bottom of the river. The oxen, frightened by having had to make the leap, and now suddenly unable to move forward a single step, stood shaking and snorting. It required all the brute strength of Steve Chalus to control them.

He commanded Elana to get in the water to retrieve the pole and reattach it to the yoke. This eternally kind and placid woman did precisely that: she waded into the ice water to her waist, worked her way forward to the front of the oxen, then immersed herself entirely to reach the pole end, and after several jerks, freed it from the river bottom. She directed the end through the ring in the yoke, where it belonged. Steve, hesitating only long enough for her to move out of the way, snapped his whip and bellowed at the oxen to move forward. Elana slowly made her way to the shore where her husband was dry and comfortable, unhitching the animals from the wagon.

Nick Woronuk had to overcome the reluctance of his team to enter the river. With the ferryman helping by striking their loins with a belt, and Nick shouting, they too finally jumped off the ferry apron into the water. Woronuk's hitch pole held and the animals proceeded to the shore. The Smoky River was crossed.

The ferryman told them that they had come just in time. The ice would get worse and he would be pulling the ferry out until an ice bridge could be built. There would be no crossing the Smoky River until at least mid-December.

"But we have three more wagons resting for a few days," Nick said.

"It depends on the ice," he replied. "If it gets worse, there will be no crossing until there is an ice bridge. That means the river has to freeze across, and then we will pump water over the thin ice to strengthen it. Only then will crossing be allowed."

As they drove off, Nick explained these conditions of river crossing to the wives. Elana panicked.

"My God," she cried out, "don't you understand? Domka is due to have her baby in mid-December. That will be impossible! They must get across!"

They stopped the oxen to discuss this critical matter. After some deliberation, Nick turned his wagon around and decided to go back to Sturgeon Lake and prompt the Lazoruk and Sandul wagons to cross the river as soon as possible.

When he reached the water's edge, the empty ferry had returned to the opposite side and the ferryman was nowhere in sight. Nick and Erena waited for some time, but there was no sign of him. They turned the oxen around again and went on to meet the Chalus wagon and proceed to Grande Prairie.

A decision was made that if the Lazoruk and Sandul wagons could not cross, they would have Domka walk across the ice to one of their wagons, and take her to Grande Prairie to have the baby. The ice would be thick enough for foot traffic earlier than for oxen and wagons. They would wait at their homestead locations until December 1, and if the wagons had not appeared by then, they would begin to retrace their way to the river. It was not a good plan, they all agreed, but it was the only one that was workable.

Slowly the oxen traversed the steep banks leading from the river. So different from Southern Manitoba, they noted, where the rivers do not create deep banks. The timber was heavy on either side of the trail, but the roadbed was free of stumps and obstacles that would have reminded them of their weeks on the Edson Trail.

When they reached the top, they could see for long distances. The terrain was nearly flat and the road relatively smooth; Erena and George crept back to the driver's seat that they had not sat on for days. Ahead, Elana, their son William, and Steve were sitting three abreast on their wagon seat. It was a comforting sight: two families on the way to their future. The scene could only have been more pleasant if the other three wagons were there.

The snow had either melted, or less of it had fallen; the sun was bright and a trickle of water from the melt was dribbling on each side of the road. Land that had been cultivated, a few acres here and a few there, was jet black, just like they had left in Bukovina.

The tribulations of the Edson-Grande Prairie Trail, the starvation, the loss of their cow, the extreme exertion needed to cross from one improbable barrier to the next; it was all in the past. When Erena referred to a trying episode on the trail, Nick would philosophize, "Forget the past, Erena. Look at that land! Ours will be the same. It will be hard work but we'll do well. We'll have children; our neighbors will be the same people that we are with now. How can life be better?" For the first time in a while, he whistled.

The sun was beginning to set in the west and a chill of the November evening was descending upon the two wagons and their occupants. Erena had Nick stop the oxen as she moved back into the box where there was more shelter. As she stood up, she caught a glimpse of a settlement, just over the tops of the trees no more than a few miles away.

"Could that be Grande Prairie?" she asked,

Nick stood in the seat and looked where she pointed.

"Yes, it sure is," he replied, a broad smile stretching across his face. "We have made it across the Edson-Grande Prairie Trail! We are alive and well, and the rest of the road to our homestead is no different than this.

"We have made it, Erena!"

# PART III

# CHAPTER 24

The two Lazoruk wagons and the wagon that Fred Sandul drove remained settled near Sturgeon Lake. The oxen and the cattle were feeding in the meadow and the wagons still contained some hay that the men had collected from the mailman's stack. The health of the animals was steadily improving; they did not need to lie down as frequently, and when they could feed normally, Nick Lazoruk predicted that they then would have regained sufficient strength to complete the trip.

On the third day, Nick decided those conditions were met. They hitched the oxen to the wagons, broke camp, and proceeded on the road westward. That evening they arrived at the Smoky River.

The ferryman was there making preparations for pulling the ferry out of the water for the winter. Mike Lazoruk explained to him their need to cross, but he said there was too much ice and they would have to wait for an ice bridge. When they asked how long they would have to wait, he said that usually they had an ice bridge by Christmas.

Mike pointed to his pregnant wife and pleaded with the ferryman to make one more trip, but he was totally disinterested. He finally stood up from what he was doing and walked away to his cabin upstream. The group stood there dumbfounded. They could not wait a month under any circumstances and, considering Domka's advanced pregnant state, there was no question that somehow they had to cross.

The first consideration was to drive the oxen across, but the stream was too swift and the animals, although having regained some strength, were not yet in condition for this task. Fred Sandul said he thought he could run the ferry. They would wait until the light went out in the cabin, drive their teams onto the deck and Fred would commence the operation. Both Nick and Mike looked at each other, fully aware that this was the young man's fantasy; however, there were no other options. They had stolen hay from the government, now they were going to steal its ferry!

Other than the experience that Mike had on their expedition in the spring, and the earlier crossing on the Athabasca River, none had any experience on ferries. The men returned to their wagons and explained the state of affairs to their wives.

Domka suggested aggression to force the ferryman to take them, but the men were reluctant to use such threats for fear of being arrested later. It seemed to them that stealing a ferry to save a pregnant woman and her baby would be better tolerated.

Under the cover of darkness, they edged their oxen carefully down the embankment and aligned them to fit three teams on the ferry. Then they loaded the cows behind the wagons. The total load was well in excess of what the ferry was designed to carry even in good water conditions. Each took a deep breath as Fred Sandul turned the crank that would angle the ferry to catch the current.

The ferry began to move into the stream. Nick and Mike took poles and pushed against the river bottom to maintain an angle that would slowly bring them to the other side. But ice was building up on the upstream side, and even using all their strength, they were having trouble keeping the angle constant. They needed to yell to Fred to crank the other way, but they did not want to alert the ferryman. Mike ran to the front with his pole and tried to push the ice away from the upstream side of the ferry, but it was building faster than he could keep it off. Nick, meanwhile, was using all the strength he had to prevent the ferry from rotating front to back, possibly breaking the cable and careening them downstream to Lord knows where.

The cable strained, and they cringed at the telltale sound of stretching wire, a low moan that could not be mistaken for anything other than wire reaching its tension limit before snapping. The children were asleep in their respective wagon boxes and the women left them there to help the men. Because of her state, Domka was delegated to pass information in low tones to Fred who was cranking the control wheel one way, then the other, hoping upon hope to find the ideal position to continue to move this monster load across the river.

On an overloaded ferry in the middle of the night, the opposite side of the river only visible as a faint dark outline, these obstacles would have presented a challenge for an expert operator. Obviously, the ferryman knew what he was talking about: the ice was treacherous; and the ferry would have had serious trouble even in daylight.

They were hardly over the midpoint of the river when there was a grinding noise from the underside of the ferry. They had struck a gravel shoal, anchoring a pivot point on the underside of the ferry. In a panic, Mike called to Fred, "Turn the other way! Hurry! We're in a spin!" It was too late. The current and the ice caught the downstream side of the ferry and rotated it 180 degrees. Now the oxen and the wagons were facing the shore they had left and their tails facing the intended bank.

The cables had twisted and were subject to snapping from the force of floating ice building against the ferry surface. The women were hysterical; the men were struggling frantically to clear the ice. The scene was more chaotic than any mud holes on the Edson Trail. The situation presented a threat to their survival, and they all knew it.

Exhausted, they finally stopped their futile struggle. There was only one option: they had to unhitch their oxen and force them into the water, then drive them around the ferry, and then drag the wagons backwards to the shore. It was a desperate plan, but there were no alternatives. There was urgency too; if the cables broke, the ice could push the ferry off the river bottom carrying them onto logjams or rocks — a potential for loss of life.

They had managed to force the ferry to within about thirty yards from shore, about three quarters of the way across the river, but there was no way of knowing how deep the water was between the shoal on which they were anchored and the shore. There was no time to waste. With the three wagons and the cattle, there was no room to turn the oxen around and unload them from the rear apron of the ferry that was closest to the shore. They had to unload toward the middle of the river, where their poles showed the depth of the water to be over three feet.

They dropped the unloading apron, unhitched the Mike Lazoruk team, and tried to drive them into the water. The oxen advanced to the edge of the apron and halted. Their eyes widened and their movements became erratic. Each animal attempted to turn around, but the yoke prevented it. They tugged at each other, snorted, and the commotion on the apron seemed to be out of control. Nick Lazoruk walked to the front of the apron, up to his knees in ice water, and pacified the animals as only he could do.

Still the oxen would not leave the ferry apron. Mike and Fred had to resort to what they later referred to as the Chalus technique. They whipped the oxen and finally the two animals leaped into the river. Mike jumped in too, holding the reins, and steered them around the ferry and to the shore. Fred Sandul was next, and with less persuasion was able to get his animals to shore. Nick Lazoruk's team only needed a command to follow.

The cattle had been loaded on the back of the ferry and tied to the wagons. The men dropped the loading apron facing the shore, turned the cattle around, and one by one, led them to land.

With the weight of the oxen and cattle removed, the ferry floated off the shoal and was swinging from side to side, like a bob on the end of a pendulum, further terrifying the women. If the cable broke then, they would be alone without a man on board, and at the mercy of the river. The men hurriedly tied the animals to trees and waded back to the ferry. Despite its reversed attitude they were able to pole it closer to shore and were now only twenty feet from the ramp. There they became stuck again and no further movement was possible.

The men tied ropes to the rear axles of the wagons, and the oxen dragged them backwards off the ferry. With one man managing the center pole to keep the front wheels straight, they succeeded in bringing all three wagons to shore.

Morning light was beginning to show in the East when the men had finally got their families and their gear across the Smoky River. Everyone was exhausted, and they chose to make camp and spend the day resting, perhaps not to leave until the following day.

The ferry was floating freely, suspended on its twisted cable, and still rotated a full 180 degrees. The ice would jamb up, then release. The ferry would respond by twisting, sometimes raising one corner as the ice went banging its way under it, then splash down into the water with a resounding whack. It was then that the ferryman appeared on the opposite shore.

He stood there stunned, his ferry nearly across the river from him, pitching in the current and turned halfway around. No one will know what went through his mind, what expletives he might have used to describe what he was witnessing. He was now marooned on the wrong side of the river, and he would have to wait until the river had frozen over to cross! It would be spring before he could rescue what remained of his ferry following a winter of icing and a spring thaw. Unquestionably, this transport unit would be a write-off, and even the guide cable to the ferry would break from the stresses of ice and water. He would have to explain the whole episode to some commission from the Government; he might be fired. He was in trouble and he knew it. He shouted to the men to bring his ferry back!

Mike replied that they didn't know how to turn it around, and he reminded him that he had refused to take them across the night before. Now they were refusing to do anything for him. The ferryman began to plead. His initial pleas fell on deaf ears, but eventually the Lazoruk men began to soften. The ferryman called to them that they would not be able to right the ferry; they would have to take the attached boat and paddle it across. Not one of the three men had ever paddled a boat.

He continued to plead with them, and apologized for his previous night's behavior. Finally Mike volunteered to take the boat and try to cross the river.

Domka, usually able to control her emotions better than any of the women, now broke down. Looking at the amount of drift ice coming downstream; having witnessed its impact on the ferry; knowing

Mike's inexperience with rowing; could he make a successful cross-ing? Unlikely!

Mike got into the boat. The ferryman shouted how to insert the oars into the oarlocks and to sit facing the back. In the lee of the ferry, the water was relatively calm and Mike practiced a few strokes to get an idea of how to move the boat and how to steer it. Then he entered the stream.

His immediate objective was to set a course straight across the river, but the battle with the ice made that plan impossible. The ice would strike the boat and half turn it around as it had done to the ferry. The ferryman shouted to let the river take him downstream; just keep pad-dling stronger with the downstream paddle and he would reach the other shore.

When Mike understood the message, he began to paddle that way, ignoring the distance across. It was easier and safer. Since the shore he was headed for was behind him, he had no idea how far he was drifting downstream except by some relative relationship he gained by seeing their camp and the ferry to his left, retracting from him.

Domka crossed herself in Orthodox fashion, clearly spoke the Trinitarian formula, and uttered a few words of prayer to God to guide Mike safely. When Mike began to paddle with less concern about the shortest distance across, those on shore could see that his struggle could be successful. A sigh of relief emanated when they saw the ferryman walking rapidly downstream to where he expected Mike to land.

Mike's oars struck bottom, dug up some sand and pebbles, and he knew he had made the other side. He turned his head to see the ferry-man standing there in six inches of water, reaching to grasp the rope hanging from the bow. As he dragged the boat onto the gravel bar, he congratulated Mike on his courage. Not a word was said about having stolen the ferry. Mike did not mention it either.

Together they pushed the boat back into the water, and Mike, using a paddle, kept it away from the shore while the ferryman dragged the boat upstream well beyond the ferry ramp and nearly to his cabin. There the two of them got back in and, with the expert strokes of the ferryman, crossed the Smoky River again.

The women had made tea, and a dish full of cooked fish and using whatever other food they had, they made a well-deserved lunch. The ferryman joined to eat with them, thanked the women for the food, and Mike for risking his life, and rowed his boat to the ferry.

He grabbed the crank and deftly turned it as far as it would go to the right. The huge platform strained and creaked, but in a few moments, he spun the wheel back. The stream caught the tip of the ferry and spun it smoothly to the normal position and he was on his way back across the river.

Mike sat down; unnerved from the whole experience, and spoke of his fear, and then the need for sleep overcame him. They went to their tents for a few hours of rest.

# CHAPTER 25

I t was early afternoon when they rose, repacked their wagons, and started up the hill toward Grande Prairie. Like the Woronuk and Chalus wagons three days before, they slowly made their way upwards to the top of the long hill and witnessed the flat terrain with small acreages that had been cultivated. These lands had been homesteaded two years before, when the Edson-Grande Prairie Trail was first cut through.

The settlers that came then would have found the trail just as rough, but if they were fortunate enough to cross it without the extra burden of mud from rain and snow, it would have been difficult but not overwhelming. Many came in winter when the snow covered the stumps, and the sleighs glided easily over the trail. Some had covered their wagons like those who came west on the Oregon Trail. In fact, many were American expatriates, who had come too late to the American West to find good homestead land, and thus had chosen to brave the Edson Trail.

Heightened by the adrenalin rush that they had experienced earlier, everything seemed more vivid: the land black, the sky blue, and the talk between them spirited. They knew that the worst of the trail was behind them. By early evening they made camp for the last time before Grande Prairie, at the approximate site of the present settlement of Teepee Creek.

The cattle and the oxen fed well. Milk production began to increase and the oxen were more alert and even rambunctious. They would rub their heads against their masters and butt them gently as they were harnessing them. It was an interesting revelation: the animals clearly responded to the human spirit. When the humans were depressed, the oxen lowered their heads; they worked but without enthusiasm. When the humans were excited and happy, the behavior of the animals was the same.

It was cold at night, and the men kept their stoves going in order to keep the tents warm. The ground was frozen in the morning, the air crisp and freezing in a white fog with each exhalation. The days had become shorter, the sun rising much later and setting much earlier than they had become accustomed to in southern Manitoba.

They were experiencing the North, and it would get even more dramatic in a month. Just around Christmas on this *Canadian calendar*, as they called it, they would experience the shortest day of the year. (In Eastern Orthodox tradition, these families adhered to the Julian calendar for religious observances and used the Gregorian calendar for all other applications.)

The train of three wagons reached the Grande Prairie settlement in the late afternoon. Grande Prairie in 1913 was a collection of a few log cabins, but still was the largest settlement in the Peace River Country. As such, it exercised substantial influence with the Government of Alberta. It became the site for homestead registry, and later was a key player in influencing railway construction to abandon a bed already prepared for rail to be built from Spirit River, Alberta, to Rolla, British Columbia. Instead, the track was laid southward from the Spirit River Settlement to serve Grande Prairie. The Edson-Grande Prairie Trail, too, had been constructed to serve this little community when other access routes were considered significantly better suited.

The price of food was high compared to Edson, Edmonton, and especially Winnipeg. The cost of transporting store supplies was excessive by either the Edson Trail or by riverboat on the Peace River to Dunvegan, and the retailers had to pass that cost on to the unfortunate consumer. The Lazoruks bought only the absolute essentials.

Two days later, they passed the little Spirit River Settlement and approached a clearing on which they recognized the Woronuk's tent. Erena saw the wagons coming, knew them well, and was waiting at the trail as they approached. There was jubilation at seeing the families again, knowing that Domka would be in a safer place to deliver her child, and that they would be together to face the winter. Steve Chalus found good soil a mile east of the Woronuk homestead, and settled as a squatter until such time as he could legitimately file for a homestead. Mike was anxious to show Domka the fine land he had selected, so they spent only a few minutes with Erena.

Nick and Erena, carrying George, walked north the quarter mile to the Nick Lazoruk homestead. There was a little clearing of less than an acre on the bank of the Spirit River that Nick Woronuk thought would make an ideal site for their home.

Nick Lazoruk and Maria got off their wagon and left the oxen in Nick Woronuk's hands while the two walked around the area. They peered down the slope to the west to see the Spirit River flowing quietly below, and another slope to the south where the river once had coursed. Nick was carrying a spade and dug through the frozen surface. The spade flipped up beautiful black soil. He repeated the process several more times and the result was the same: black productive soil, and not a rock in sight. The land was worth the effort it took to reach it. Maria and he smiled — they agreed on the site for their home. The older children were already racing around stretching their legs and warming themselves from the chill of that November day. What was most rewarding was that they would not have to pack up the next morning or any morning thereafter. This was to be their home.

Erena, with George, stayed to help Maria with hungry children and setting up their tent for the final time. Nick Woronuk walked another three-quarters of a mile north to Mike Lazoruk's chosen site. It too sat on the bank of the Spirit River, on a natural clear area, no more than 50 yards from the trail. Domka, now a month from her due date, was struggling with her two children, in need of rest and a stable place to wait out her pregnancy. Nick helped Mike set up their tent and get the fire going, and Mike took a pail and axe to cut a trail through to the river.

Ice was forming along the edges of the stream. Beavers had fallen poplar and the downed trees were forming bridges over the water. From one, Mike reached in and filled his pail with crystal clear water. This would be the site for all the water they would use for years to come.

It was dark when they finished the necessary preparations for their last unloading. Domka had made tea, and the good friends sat down to talk about their urgent responsibilities. There was immediate agreement that they must build a log cabin for Domka, which they would start in the morning. Instead of going directly home, Nick walked to Steve Chalus's home site to ask him to come to help Mike build, and then he stopped in to see Nick Lazoruk as well. Fred Sandul said he would stay a day, and help and then walk back to Edson to take a train home to Manitoba. He was particularly anxious to get to Grande

Prairie and file for a homestead for his father and another for himself. They had seen the land office busy with settlers and had followed a few wagons going north to the Spirit River area. Land was being taken up rapidly.

The next morning at daybreak, the men gathered at Mike Lazoruk's place and began selecting trees with straight trunks that were minimally tapered in order to stack tightly for the walls of a small log shack. They chose aspen poplar because the sap would have gone down into the roots for the winter and these trees, they speculated, would be dryer than the spruce.

Nick Woronuk and Fred Sandul were the only men inexperienced in log house building. Nick was an expert as a tree cutter but the intricate notching of the corners he would learn from the other men as they began to assemble the logs. In one day the five men had cut enough logs for a small cabin and skidded them, using Mike's oxen team, to the building site.

Seeing that the cabin would require a type of work that he was unable to do, Fred Sandul said good-bye to the settlers and headed back to Grande Prairie to file for homesteads and then retrace the trail on foot to Edson. He borrowed a pack board from Nick Woronuk and a small caliber pistol from Mike Lazoruk. Everyone helped supply food for this youngster with the courage of a much older man. He took off at a trot, and as far as they could see, he continued trotting until he disappeared into bush. Fred must have maintained that pace. He was back in Edson in only eight days, including having spent a part of a day registering homesteads. Unfortunately, the closest land available was some four miles to the northeast of the Mike Lazoruk place. All the land along the Spirit River, so valuable because it provided an assured water supply, was taken up from the time Nick and Mike had made their initial trip in the spring. Fred and his family would return in the spring of 1914, as homesteaders, and their land would remain in the family name for a century.

# CHAPTER 26

Mike had noticed a wagon carrying a group of three native men stopped on the trail near his building site. The men in the wagon seemed mute, simply standing in their wagon watching Mike's oxen skid the logs from the riverbank. They were still there after two trips, and to him they appeared immobile in their positions. It was an interesting sight: no audible communication, no visible changes in position, only their horses showed some impatience. Mike needed hay for feed for the winter; the horses they were using were obviously well fed, and he thought the natives might have hay for sale. He walked over to them. They did shuffle a bit as he came near, and the driver seemed the one designated to do the talking. "You got hay for sale?" Mike asked.

"Much," came the one word reply.

"How much money?"

"No want money. Whiskey trade."

"Wait," Mike said as he turned to walk back to the tent. He had brought a few bottles of Hudson's Bay rum from Grande Prairie because he knew from experience in Sturgeon Lake that this was an excellent bartering product. Mike returned with a bottle of rum, opened the cap and handed it to the driver. He took more than a healthy swig, coughed and gasped a bit, wiped his mouth on the cuff of his coat then took another swallow or two. Tears came to his eyes and his voice came through as a wheeze, his vocal cords constricted by the shock of alcohol. Now there was hyperactivity from the others in the wagon... a complete transformation from the moments before the bottle arrived. Obviously, the other men were anxious to test the bottle's contents.

"Good whiskey," the native struggled to say. "Go to trail," he continued as he pointed to his left, "turn into bush trail to hay. Help yourself." There were no suggestions of how far to go or how much hay was there, but this was the native way of communicating: no direction of north or south, simply follow trails. Mike wondered if he would find the hay and whether there was enough for the cost of the rum he had bartered.

That evening, Nick Woronuk and Mike took their wagons and drove in the direction the native had indicated. Sure enough, around two miles up the trail was another wagon track into the bush, and a short distance in were several stacks of excellent hay, well dried and tightly packed into domes to shed water. They loaded their wagons with a winter's supply of hay and enough to use as thatching for the roof of Mike's shack.

Financially, the advantage was clearly in Mike's favor, but the good time the wagonload of natives had that night was probably unsurpassed, and could not be measured in dollars and cents.

An amicable relationship was established in the native's mind that would prove problematic to Mike for months. The native showed no reluctance to visit Mike Lazoruk thereafter, trading whatever he had for whiskey, including, in one instance, beautifully embroidered moccasins right off his feet. It was a serious problem to Mike and Domka because they soon had no more liquor to trade, but the visits continued, sometimes interrupting them while asleep. It was spring before this pattern ceased.

Mike and his brother Nick notched the logs at the corners just as they had done when building the church at Arbakka. This was a time consuming and meticulous procedure, fitting the notch to the adjacent notch to reduce the space imperfections and produce a powerful joint at the same time. For the sake of time, the walls were to be only around six feet high. Rafters were built from lodge pole pine because of its strength and straightness. In ten days they had the shack built except the covering for the roof. Domka and her two children moved from the tent into the cabin so that the men could use the tent canvas to cover the roof and the stove to warm the interior. Meanwhile they selected the best of their hay for thatching.

Thatching is a process of tying the hay into tight bundles to reduce water penetration. These bundles are then arranged in the same fashion as shingles, layering so that when the roof is complete, it is waterproof and the hay provides excellent insulation. In a day or two, Mike had the roof complete and what remained to be done in the winter months was to plaster between the logs on the inside of the cabin to prevent draft and frost from penetrating to the inside.

Elana, Maria, and Erena all gathered for the *klaka*, a term used to describe a communal effort to assist in a service where the more hands, the better. Men dug frozen clay, and collected manure and grass and straw to make the plaster for Domka's walls. Despite the ice water, frozen clay and cold manure, the women took off their stockings and mixed the mass with bare feet, just as Italians were known to do in squashing grapes for wine making.

Two women would mix for a while, then one would be spelled off to warm her feet. Domka was not excluded; she took her turn with the rest of them, her belly bouncing up and down like a basketball in the hands of an expert dribbler. There was laughter, teasing, and gossip, and at the end of the day, Domka's shack had all the log chinks sealed from the inside. The wind could no longer blow through and the shack was becoming cozy.

December and January are the coldest months of the year in the Peace River Country, and temperatures can drop to -60° F (-50° C). A warm environment for a newborn is a survival necessity. The four families were well aware of the risks of such cold that could descend any day now, and they rushed to provide adequate shelter for the Mike Lazoruk family. Steve Chalus, Elana, and son William chose to stay the winter in their tent. Nick Lazoruk, with Maria and their four children, Lena, Steve, Dora, and Alyce did the same. They banked the outside of their tents with hay and snow to prevent drafts from occurring, and they were comfortable all winter.

On December 22, in her shack, attended by Wasylena, everyone's choice for a midwife, Domka gave birth to a son whom they named John. John had to be a healthy baby, having survived the Edson Trail, and born in a shack built from green timber, plastered with mud, manure, and straw—humid like a sauna. He would boast all his life that he was an Edson Trail survivor who had never seen the Edson Trail! A consummate comedian, he lived for a life with laughter.

A mile south, the Woronuk family was living in a tent, but Nick was building a shack as well. His axe skills were well honed, and he flattened two opposite surfaces of each log he set. The fit was better but progress was slow. There was urgency to finish the project because he would have to leave for Edson with the other men to bring back the farm implements they had left there.

By the first of January, the walls of the shack were up, and the rafters set for a single room with a clay floor. Like Mike Lazoruk during the plastering process, Nick had to use the tent and stove to cover the roof to warm the area, so that the mud, manure, and straw mix would not freeze. He had previously dug a cave in the side of the bank to provide shelter for the oxen. Without a stove and tent, the family moved into the cave with the oxen. The animals' natural heat made the cave remarkably comfortable, although without light.

By January 7, 1914, Nick Woronuk had finished thatching the roof. He moved the family from the cave to a little log structure with six-foot walls and a sloped roof. The camp stove that was used while crossing the Edson Trail doubled as a cook stove and heating unit. A black stovepipe rose, and as it passed through the roof, it was plastered in to separate the pipe from the flammable hay.

Heating the shack was not difficult; to take it from near freezing temperature to a cozy warm took but a few minutes once the fire was going. But such a system required constant attention because the stovepipe could become extremely hot, or embers could settle on the thatch and cause the roof to ignite. Many trappers and settlers suffered this cause of fire, and it sometimes resulted in loss of life.

In the spring, Nick planned to replace the hay roof with grass sod that was less flammable, but digging it from the frozen ground was not possible in the winter. Once the plastered floor had dried, it was much like ceramic tile, but warmer to walk on. Erena frequently spoke of the wonders of her log shack despite its many shortcomings.

Its major problem stemmed from the green logs from which it was built. Erena suffered the same problems that Domka was having—the heating of the shack during the day would cause the moisture in the wood to condense, and the walls would become soaking wet. At night, when the fire in the stove was low and the interior temperature dropped, the walls would conduct the cold from the outside, and the moisture would freeze into a glistening ice sheath from the roof to the floor. Then, the following morning, with the room warming, the ice would melt and drip into pools on the floor creating a muddy surface around the entire interior perimeter of the shack. It made a mess, but it was shelter, and there was the constant hope for better conditions in the future.

# CHAPTER 27

D ecember days in the North are short. In the Spirit River area, at the winter solstice, the sun rises at 9:30 a.m. and sets by 4:30 p.m. When the sun does rise, it skims across the southern horizon, and its rays strike this part of the world, covered in a blanket of snow, like a flat rock thrown to skip off a water surface. The light travels through countless miles of atmosphere at that angle and its heat impact is minimized. The winter months are cold.

There were almost no vegetables to eat during this first winter, the only meat was rabbit and ruffed grouse, neither animal having any substantial fat, and Nick and Erena had no cow to provide milk. They were eating animal protein but their bodies were starving for the essential nutrients that were lacking in such a diet. In that respect, they were worse off than the other families who had milk to supplement their meat diet.

As Maria's breast milk was naturally diminishing, Erena carried George in her arms a mile through snow and bitter cold to the Chalus family to get access to milk that they were able to spare. George, now sixteen months old, was walking, about the same state he had been in while still in Manitoba four months before.

In January, the four men harnessed their oxen for the return trip to Edson to retrieve the implements they had stored with the blacksmith. They took the wagon boxes off the wheeled wagons and repositioned them on their sleighs. Despite having to tolerate the cold, the snow made travel easier. The mud holes that had given them such problems in November were frozen over and covered with a thick blanket of snow. The sleighs drifted effortlessly over the surface. The oxen could pull all day with minimum fatigue, and the hay that they carried lasted the thirteen days it took to travel the trail back to Edson. They had realized that winter travel, despite the cold, was the appropriate time to make the trek.

Their machinery was still in place for them to pick up. They explained their tribulations to the blacksmith, and he admitted that he had been planning to dispose of their equipment in the spring. The mailman had told him that he doubted that their group would survive the obstacles before them. By mid-February, they were back with their families and the move completed.

It was a lonely time for the women when the men were away; with children, they were confined to their cabins or tents. The days were short and darkness set in early. The children went to sleep, and the mothers stayed up to keep the heater burning for warmth.

Often on clear nights Erena sat outside the shack, observing the starlit sky. She was fascinated by the movement of star patterns, and learned to identify visible constellations and predict *heavenly traffic*, as she called it, throughout her life. She forecasted the times that meteors would dance across the sky and even noted what may have been comets that appeared periodically. Remarkable observational memory and excellent vision made her the local authority on celestial dynamics.

But Erena's free time was not dedicated to star gazing alone. This was her opportunity to delve into the miracle of reading. Nick had left some letters and old newspapers at home, and these constituted her library. She practiced reading them, and when he returned, she amazed him with her advanced reading skill. She then began to study his handwriting, to learn to write as well. Although the writing did not progress as rapidly as reading, she was able to form many words in Cyrillic, mimicking her husband's meticulous handwriting. In time, her reading and writing skills were equivalent to an advanced grade school student.

When the men returned, there was cause for celebration. The four families got together in one home, and stories were related well into the night. The families drew ever closer together. Although destitute, they found great pleasure in each other's company. Nick Woronuk would bring out his violin and play the tunes they all knew, and the women sang along as the men clapped their hands.

Winter was passing and soon the weather would begin to warm. The daily routine continued: there was firewood to cut, animals to feed, and water to bring up from the Spirit River by pail to bathe, cook and clean. As the days lengthened, there was time left for the men to cut brush to prepare land for cultivation. The frozen bush cut easily, and by the time the weather had begun to warm, the men had cleared a few acres that they would be able to plow when the frost came out of the ground.

# CHAPTER 28

S pring was in the air, and Erena succumbed to a driving urge to raise chickens. Nick went to a neighbor, a Metis, whose wife had chickens, and asked to buy eggs and a setting hen. They agreed on a dozen fertilized eggs, and the rental of a setting hen for three weeks, for a substantial fee of $2.00.

It was April 1914 when Nick brought the setting hen and eggs to an excited Erena. She immediately made a nest in the corner of the shack and tried to persuade the hen to accept the eggs and begin the setting process. The hen obstinately refused and wandered around the room for hours, satisfying her setting instinct by clucking and setting on one object or another, but avoiding the eggs entirely. Within days, Erena had so domesticated the hen that she could pick her up at will, reset her on the eggs, pet her, and treat her like royalty.

Finally, on the fifth day, the hen got the idea. She sat over the eggs, fussing and turning them periodically, as a brood hen should, and used her body heat to keep the eggs warm. Even George was rushed outside during crying spells in order not to disturb this surreal atmosphere.

Precisely three weeks after the transaction, a tall young man knocked on the door. Nick opened it. Standing there was the son of the family from whom he had rented the hen, requesting her return. All the pleading to allow the hen to set for the five days she had been on strike, did not alter the young man's purpose. The contract time was up; he came to claim his parents' hen. There was no room for negotiation — a deal was a deal. Erena, nearly in tears, lifted the hen from the eggs and gave her to the young man. He left without further conversation, hen tucked under his arm, and took the shortest route home.

Necessity, it is said, is the mother of invention. Five more days and the eggs would have hatched. Without body heat, the embryos would die in a matter of hours. Erena carried the nest, covered with a blanket, from one place in the room to another, trying to find a location that would simulate the warmth of the hen. No location seemed to provide the incubation temperature that she knew was essential. In desperation, she bared her abdomen, tied a sheet of cloth around it, spread the eggs in a pouch in the sheet and let her body heat provide the necessary warmth. She sent Nick to ask her mother, Wasylena, to come to help in caring for George, who still needed to be carried occasionally.

Nick chuckled to himself as he walked to the Nick Lazoruk tent. How was he to relate his dilemma to his mother-in-law? But he did it with a twinkle in his eye, a characteristic Wasylena knew only too well. He dramatized the disastrous state of his household and asked for her help. "Mother," he started, "I have a problem in our house that only you can solve. Your daughter—my wife—thinks she is a brooding hen!"

He stopped, and waited for these words to sink in. A little twitch quivered at the corners of his mouth, and the crow's feet deepened around his eyes, a telltale sign of his character. "She has taken the eggs that the hen was setting on and wrapped them around her belly! In five days she will not only be the mother of her son, but a dozen chicks as well." Then he finally admitted that the hen was reclaimed, and that this was an alternative invented by Erena, but at the expense of not being able to carry George when he needed attention.

After a lengthy chuckle, Wasylena did not hesitate. She, like her daughter, knew the value of raising domestic chickens, and she came every morning and stayed all day looking after George, while her nineteen year old daughter played the part of a setting hen. At night, Erena would carefully distribute the eggs amongst the sleepers, under down quilts; the eggs remained warm enough that hatching occurred on time. Erena had a brood of twelve chicks, the first of any of the four families. She was rightfully proud, and the first component of a successful farming venture was achieved. It would be the subject of many reminiscences over the years.

The chicks had never seen a hen. They assumed the living beings in the shack must indeed be their parents. George and Erena, and to a lesser degree, Nick, were to become surrogate parents to a brood of chicks. They remained in the shack for a few weeks while they lost their chick down and became feathered. George would prance around the room with the chicks willfully following him. If he sat on the ground, they would climb over his legs and up his shirt. Erena carefully instructed the little boy to not abuse her brood.

The month of May arrived. The days were long, and the snow was almost gone; patches of grass were greening and Erena was anxious to introduce the chicks to the outdoors, and to the wonders of insects and seeds that they would discover.

On a particularly sunny morning, she removed the barrier to the chicks that she had placed against the door, and holding George by one hand, she stepped outside. The chicks, as was their habit, followed her. The fresh air, the sunshine, the grass underfoot was a delightful experience, and they chirped their appreciation louder than ever. Their necks bent near the ground, they scurried in short dashes in every direction, ecstatic in their newfound environment.

But Erena and her son were not the only witnesses to this occurrence. High above them were eyes with binocular-like vision, born to survive by capitalizing on just such a moment. With wings set into a steep dive, the purring sound of disturbed air turned to a roar as the great raptor, its legs extended, its talons curled, seized a chick but two feet from Erena's foot, and with mighty swoops of its wings raised itself, and the hapless chick, to its nest somewhere in the forest near the river.

The boldness of this bird of prey was astonishing. Wild birds were wild; they kept their distance from humans, but hawks like this one had no fear. As it flew away it squawked an eerie shriek that must have signaled its brood that dinner was available, for a few moments later, Erena looked up to see several more above her in the sky. Before she could round up the little chicks and persuade them to follow her into the house, she had lost two more.

She told Nick her sad story that evening. He went to the Doc Calkin store at the Spirit River Settlement to buy chicken wire. Doc Calkin was there that day, and Nick bought sufficient to build an enclosure measuring approximately six feet square. He used four thin poles to which he attached the mesh and set it up for Erena's chickens.

It worked well…for a while. The hawks circled overhead, anxiously waiting for some chick to escape the enclosure, but none did. As the birds grew in size, Erena would move the enclosure to new sites where the grass was fresh, and they thrived. Yet, eventually, their numbers diminished. The hawks could not fly into and fly out of the small enclosure, but other predators were feeding on her chickens. The final count of salvaged chickens was five; a loss of over 50% to the marauders that raided her henhouse.

Those five chickens would produce eggs, and one became a brooder hen. The process of renewal began. In a few months, Erena raised a substantial flock of chickens, then added ducks and geese. They matured the following summer and she plucked the down from their breasts for quilts and pillows. Erena had a yard full of clucking, hissing, and quacking birds.

*Hallis "Doc" Calkin was an inspirational perplexity. He and a partner, Bill English, had settled in the Spirit River Settlement area around 1903, built a "stopping place," and ran a fur trading business and eventually a general store. Together they had leased some 5000 acres of land on which to raise horses and cattle. This was their key enterprise; the store was an aside that eventually Doc managed alone, and in a unique way. He never locked the door to the store and was rarely present to serve the few customers. Purchases were made on something resembling an honor code: the customer wrote what he took on a sheet of paper or left money for it on the counter. It was more a service to the settlers than a moneymaking enterprise for Doc. The name "Calkin" still resonates in the minds of those who remember him. He was one of the truly gracious and benevolent people who helped the community get established.*

In the mornings, while George slept, Erena rose from bed and tiptoed from the shack to the garden plot to begin digging the soil. With each spadeful she turned up black rock-free earth. The plot had not been cultivated before and was overgrown with grass and weeds. She methodically shook the rich soil from the roots and piled the weeds for burning later.

Erena was in her element. What sort of garden would such soil produce? Waiting for it to warm sufficiently to plant taxed her patience. By the time the middle of May arrived, she had dug up a substantial garden plot, weeded it thoroughly, and had the first semblance of an established farm operation on the Woronuk homestead.

During this period, Nick had been clearing brush and some trees from a partly clear area, preparing it for the plow. He, too, was anxious to hook his oxen to the new one-bottom walking plow he had brought from Edson, and see what the furrow would show. The time finally arrived. He had cleared about two acres of brush and trees, cut the roots free to turn the stumps upward, and piled them for burning after they dried. Erena followed him to the patch he had selected: it was four times larger than what he would have inherited in Onut from his father's plot.

On the first strikeout, Erena drove the oxen while Nick managed the new plow angle to gauge the depth of the furrow. Both were excited; would the plow reveal rocks like Manitoba, or would it produce the black loam that Erena had uncovered in her garden? Erena urged the oxen forward when Nick told her he was ready. He guided the plow shear into the homestead soil and the first furrow began to form.

It was black!

Black as tar!

It folded into a perfect furrow, exposing the undermined roots of the vegetation to the sun and wind to dry, and readied it for harrows, and then seed. No moment in their lives together was as profound as the realization that they had truly found what it was they suffered so much to find: soil that was like that which they imagined to have been in the Garden of Eden.

They stopped the oxen at the end of the strikeout and walked back a bit to examine the furrow. Both marveled at what they saw. They had made the first plowed area together. From here on, Nick would manage alone by guiding the oxen with voice calls, the lines tied behind his back, his hands free to control the depth of the furrow that the plow shear was making.

By the middle of May, Erena found waiting for spring overwhelming. She had to plant, though the nights were still cool with temperatures around the freezing mark. She planted the few seed potatoes that she had resolutely saved even while starving on the Edson Trail. She had also brought seeds for carrots and lettuce, and had already started tomatoes in the shack for seedlings to transplant in the garden, when the time was right. The garlic cloves she had buried in November, when they first arrived, were sprouting, and she had onion sets to plant as well. This would be a complete garden, and would be the first of seven gardens that she and Nick eventually tended. This one plot would produce enough food to feed her family, and some would be available for market. Erena's garden produce would be the first source of income derived from their land.

Nature has a tendency to allow a glimpse at its most exotic offering, and then expose the alternative. The soil was rich, the fowl were growing as the weather was warming — and then the mosquitoes appeared. Not the odd one, causing upset by buzzing around while you tried to sleep, but swarms of them, so thick that they partially blocked out the sun.

The garden lay a short distance from the shack, but to reach it, Erena had to break a leafed branch to swing constantly to avoid the hordes that attacked her. Even the hardy oxen were throwing their heads around in a futile attempt to rid their bodies of these vicious pests. Nick wore fleece-lined winter underwear, even in the intense heat of summer, to protect his body from mosquitoes.

Erena checked for the direction of slight breeze. Upwind from where she worked, she built a smudge: a smoke producing fire of weeds and manure that produced a heavy pungent smoke that would keep the mosquitoes away. Even in the field, where Nick worked, he built smudges to give moments of respite to him and to the suffering oxen.

There were a variety of mosquitoes, depending upon the season of the year. The large dark brown ones appeared in the spring, then another variety in the summer, and finally, a small light brown variety in the fall that seemed to lay dormant in the grass until disturbed. This latter variety settled on ankles and lower legs where smoke did not provide protection.

Mosquitoes were virtually unknown in Bukovina, and they were rare even in Manitoba. Fleas were common in Manitoba, and they too posed a nuisance, but not to the degree that was caused by the savagery of the mosquitoes in the Peace River area.

As obnoxious as these pests were to humans and animals, they did not affect the growth in Erena's garden. The plantings and seedlings thrived, but the soil, still inundated with seed and roots from thousands of years of natural growth, required constant hoeing to keep weeds from overwhelming the food-bearing plants.

Erena's plants were carefully sown in straight lines facing north and south for those that required the maximum sunshine, and east and west for those that didn't. Hers was a prudent plan, one practiced by countless generations of people in Bukovina and now transferred to the Spirit River area of Alberta.

Rains came and went, and when they did not arrive on time, Erena or Nick carried water from the river, a hundred yards up to the garden plot, and manually irrigated the thirsty plants. Just as Nick had portrayed, it became a jungle, with potato leaves as *large as elephant ears*, sometimes shading out other nearby plants pleading for sunlight.

It was a summer of wonders. In a few weeks, lettuce was ready, radish too, and the makings of salads began to replenish the essential nutrients that only green plants can provide. The morning vertigo, uncharacteristic weakness, and bleeding gums soon disappeared. These were the signs of scurvy, caused by living a winter without access to fruits and vegetables. George was growing and, although pocked from mosquito bites, he was happy and healthy, thanks to the milk supply offered by Aunt Elana Chalus, whose cow still produced a little milk.

# CHAPTER 29

A cow, a replacement for Jenny, was a necessity. The Chalus cow was drying up and George, though able to eat all the foods of adults, still needed the incomparable nutrients that milk offered. Nick went to the same Metis family from whom he had bought eggs and rented the brooding hen. The family had a cattle ranch and calving season was over. There might be a cow they would sell that had calved and now produced milk. Indeed they did. They pointed to one out in the field that looked wholesome. Nick paid for the cow and asked one of the sons if he could bring the animal over. They had horses, were good horsemen, and bringing the animal would be easy for them.

Erena was happy to have a milking cow again, but she had no idea what was in store. This was no ordinary milking cow: this was a range cow that had produced calves, and had probably never had a human hand touch her. If there ever was a monster in the bovine family, this was one. The neighbor's boys brought her over using ropes tied to the horns and neck. Two good horses dragged the obstinate animal nearly a mile that also required crossing the river. They tied her up in the cave, and waved to Nick as they galloped off, leaving him to attempt to calm the puffing, struggling animal.

Every attempt to come close to this beast was met with violent jerks to the tie rope, glaring eyes, and a bellow that resembled, Nick thought, the horn sound of the Sophia Hohenberg leaving the dock at Trieste. She would spin in the stall, kick with one or both hind legs and thrash around so that any approach was futile. Erena came to see the animal, and was met with the same display of contempt for the human race that the cow had shown Nick. The two stood back and realized that milking this creature would be suicidal.

Erena suggested getting help from her brother, Nick Lazoruk, whose skill at calming animals had been demonstrated so many times on the trail. She walked over to the Lazoruk's and explained her problem. Nick, good natured and competent, walked back with her to see this animal that he presumed would be manageable with a little time and effort. He assumed his sister had exaggerated the cow's disposition to him — and then he walked to where she was tied.

The animal was in a lather. She had fought the riders for a mile and, having never experienced a rope, had fought on for more than an hour while tied to the stall. He could hear her bellow as he approached, and when he saw her antics, even Nick Lazoruk shook his head in disbelief. This was not a domesticated animal at all; this was a wild beast that might never be subdued. But the three of them would try to milk her. In his years of experience, there had never been an animal that he didn't finally tame. This was not going to be his first!

He took a length of rope from which he made a basic lasso. He dropped the loop on the floor beside her thrashing rear legs and waited. It did not take long; her flailing right leg stepped into the loop and Nick jerked the rope taut.

Normally an animal of that size, limited to standing on three legs, would be seriously incapacitated and would stand still. Not so this devil cow; she swung her head around, lost her balance, and fell to the ground. That provided kicking ability with both hind legs, even though a tight rope was restraining one leg. Nick pulled the rope tighter; with the leg now extended, he was able to throw half hitches over the slip-knot and prevent the rope from slipping off the leg. Then he released the tension and she stood up immediately. Puffing and bellowing, she did not throw herself off balance again.

With the hind right leg pulled back a foot off the ground, Nick approached her and laid his hand on her back. She squirmed, and bellowed again, but he held his ground and finally he was able to touch her udder and eventually express a bit of milk from her teats. While Nick Woronuk held the leg rope, Nick Lazoruk milked the cow. Erena, who had done all the milking of the jersey, stood back wondering how she would milk such a maniacal animal.

This milking procedure was repeated twice each day for several days. The men left the rope on the leg although they released the tension. Later, Nick Woronuk could raise the animal's leg, and Erena braved advancing to milk the cow. Nick brought water from the river and left it in a pail in the stall. He gave the cow hay for feed but she would not touch it. She was losing weight and needed the grass that she was accustomed to. Nick and Erena decided to release her from being tied to the stall, and planned to both hold the long rope as they guided her to pasture.

But the brute had different ideas. The moment she realized that she was no longer confined, she burst from the stall and raced up the hill dragging both Nick and Erena with her. A poplar tree was in the direction of her ascent, and Nick, realizing he could not contain this animal, tried to circle the rope around the tree and stop her. He never made it.

Erena had let go earlier, and Nick could not get far enough around the tree to circle it. She spun him from his half circle and the fingers of his left hand crushed against the trunk. The middle finger broke at its middle joint; a surging pain shot up his arm, and he too, let go the rope. Free of all restraint, except the dragging rope, the beast headed at full gallop for the river.

As Nick and Erena watched, she leapt into the water without a moment's hesitation, crossed to the other side, and wildly galloped up the hill to her calf and the range cattle she was familiar with. A few days later, the neighbor brought back the rope and refunded Nick his money.

Nick concluded that he was not a seasoned farmer. He learned that you investigate animals carefully before you buy them. He would be a much wiser farmer in the future.

The need for milk remained. Nick walked to another neighbor, also Metis, who had cattle. He selected a cow that had calved in the spring and was being milked daily. He petted her and she seemed docile. He led her by a neck rope and she did not balk. Erena now had a cow that she could milk, and George would have the nutrients that only milk could provide.

The fractured finger joint healed slowly, with neither a cast nor a splint to stabilize it. During healing, the most comfortable position that Nick could find was with the finger bent at about a 45° angle, and in that position, the fractured joint became immobile.

In a few weeks he was able to do all the duties necessary with little limitation from the bent finger, but violin playing presented a problem. The inflexibility of the finger in his left hand affected playing in tune. He found he could slide his index finger forward to play a half tone higher to produce the tone that should have been the responsibility of the broken finger. It was an improvisation, but it worked. When the weather was inclement, and he had some spare time, he would practice this invention until he had mastered it. Only a discerning musician would have been able to tell that he was masquerading the use of his middle finger.

Before his injury, Nick had sown his prepared plot to wheat by a method referred to as *broadcasting*. He carried a quantity of wheat in a pail and threw it randomly, with a sweeping motion, to spread it, more or less evenly, over the prepared plot. There was urgency to do this; frosts came early in the area and it was now the latter part of May.

Nick had bought some seed wheat in Grande Prairie on his return from Edson. It was a relatively new brand called Marquis, developed by the legendary Canadian agriculturist, Dr. Charles Saunders, and purported to ripen earlier than the Red Fife from which it stemmed. It is likely that this was the very first Marquis wheat to be sown in the Spirit River area. It would become the most popular wheat grown in the region for many years.

As summer approached, Nick, still having to favor his broken finger, had to tolerate the discomfort to begin building two structures: a barn for the cow and oxen and a granary to store the expected crop of wheat. The summer and fall of 1914 would bring good news and bad for the settlers of the Spirit River Settlement. They learned that the expected railroad would pass through the homestead land of Nick's father, George Woronuk. Contrarily, by fall, the British Empire had declared war on their homeland, the Austrian Empire, and on Germany.

Still, Erena's garden was growing, and she went to it in every spare moment, eradicating an occasional stubborn weed, or hurrying to the river for a pail of water to nourish a needy plant.

The mosquitos continued their obnoxious quest for blood, and smudges were constantly lit. Nick had fitted a better door on the shack, and the glass that he bought in Grande Prairie became windows on the east and west. Erena called another *klaka*, and the women plastered the outside of the shack. That helped insulate against the heat of the summer and the cold of winter. George was gurgling phrases and desperately trying to participate in adult conversation. Everyone was responding to his animated garble, and he showed pride in being recognized amongst adults.

# CHAPTER 30

Britain declared war on Germany moments after midnight on August 4, 1914. Canada followed on the succeeding day. A week later, the British Empire declared war on Austro-Hungary. When the news reached the Spirit River area, several of the young early settlers of British heritage immediately enlisted to fight for "King and Country." Most had penetrated into the Peace River before the Edson Trail had been cut. They were hardy men, ranchers primarily; some had built up substantial herds of cattle and horses. Their dedication to their motherland was noteworthy, but what they faced in the next four years defies description.

Few returned, and of those that did, most were physically or psychologically compromised. Young Metis men also enlisted, not for their love of Britain, but for the spirit of adventure that only wars seem able to provide. It was disruptive to the little settlement. Good neighbors were gone, their stock sometimes sold at low prices, or their older kin stayed on, determined to maintain the ranch until their sons returned. It was, after all, going to be a brief skirmish so the press emphatically predicted.

But the war brought insidious changes in attitudes to the social structure throughout Canada. These new settlers were Austrians, even spoke some German, dressed differently, ate different food, and worshiped an odd faith. They were an identifiable minority, and the first elements of discrimination emerged.

Incidents of it had occurred over the years: the indifferent, hostile attitude of the Canadian Immigration officer in Trieste, and the occasional local semblance of disgust, when language became a barrier to understanding. But these rare instances had been overlooked because of the generosity of so many. There had been the gift of money from a total stranger in New York; Stanley in Manitoba; the men in the lumber camps outside Winnipeg: countless events that shaded the exceptions into virtual obscurity. Now, the same neighbors that had previously been ready to communicate and to share, with their sons gone to support their British motherland, began to shun the immigrants of Austro-Ukrainian descent. It was disconcerting yet meaningless in the beginning, but it was to grow to frightening proportions. The First World War was to prove not a brief encounter but one of the world's greatest catastrophes.

Some young men that had walked the trail through the Woronuk and Lazoruk lands now struggled in the mud of France and choked on poison gas at Ypres. Instead of returning to their homesteads, their remains were buried in the soils of foreign countries. Canada adopted the War Measures Act, and arrested over 8000 recent Ukrainian speaking immigrants from Austro-Hungary, stripping them of their possessions and interring them into forced labor camps.

The seeds of prejudice were sown by the very act of war, and an ethnically definable enemy. As the conflict wore on, and the news that

yet another local British-Canadian soldier was lost forever, simple discrimination grew into racism, and the four families felt its full force. It
would continue to grow throughout the war years, and when the dis-
ruption of that worthless struggle would be assessed, heritage became
a profound issue. The expletive, *Bohonk,* a derogation of the already
uncomplimentary form of Bohemian, resounded in the local vernacular. The term was particularly unnerving to the settlers. Unfamiliar
with an environment that contrasted with the acceptance to which
they had become accustomed, they withdrew more into their ethnic
group, and centered their attention on the customs and traditions they
had brought with them from Bukovina.

No matter how small a gathering, within it will be found a revolutionary. In these four families, the vivacious Erena was clearly a
nonconformist. Following a discussion regarding the discriminatory
environment they were confronting, she discarded her cloth headdress,
a hair covering of early Christian tradition and Orthodox dogma that
distinguished a woman of faith.

In the same severance from her traditions, she had already quit
embroidering; something, which from childhood she'd considered a
waste of valuable time. She continued to cherish the beautiful designs
on Ukrainian costume clothing, but chose to wear common clothing
that was indistinguishable from women of other cultures.

These were bold steps. In the eyes of her mother and older sister
Elana, not covering her hair, bordered on heresy. How could a woman,
married and a mother, so expose herself? If they had a pastor he would
threaten her with damnation; her child would suffer, her plants would
wither and die! This simple act had countless consequences.

But Erena saw her George healthy and robust, her plants thrive, and
no untoward consequences descended on her. Superstitions had little
influence on her. She depended on rational and observable criteria to

guide her, but if such criteria negatively affected a happy, productive life, they were discarded. Obstinate, she stuck to her principles and faced, for a time, not only isolation from her British neighbors, but also from her own mother and older sister as well.

Maria, always the patient one, neither condoned nor objected to Erena's conversion, and Domka, outspoken and discerning, supported Erena yet kept with her ethnic traditions. Nick took little notice. Involved with his farm development, and accustomed to seeing his wife without headdress in the privacy of their home life, her new mode was but an extension of that period of time. Nick Lazoruk and Mike simply laughed at their sister, and Steve Chalus expressed no interest at all. He might never have noticed, buried in his work as he was. This man rarely saw what existed above the level of the horizon. His unmatched commitment to labor was a wonder to all who knew him.

Ridding herself of the historic traditions of her Slavic heritage did little to endear her to those who sneered at the struggling families. "Internally," Erena said, "I felt a powerful feeling of emancipation, as though an obscuring cloud had drifted from me, and the sun shone through." It was in her nature: she would lead in acts of rational judgment throughout her life, opening avenues of opportunity both for her family, and for the more passive relatives in the settlement.

Nick's wheat was growing tall and heading out, and he strove to contain the weeds. He walked carefully, stepping between the random wheat stalks to pluck weeds from the ground. Working through hours of daylight that extended from five in the morning until ten at night, one might find Nick building the barn or the granary. Yet however remarkable his work ethic was, Steve Chalus was up earlier, worked later, and, probably with his inexhaustible endurance, he worked harder. Nick and Mike Lazoruk equaled Nick Woronuk, but none could match the driven Steve Chalus.

In August the wheat began to yellow. There was going to be a great yield from the two acres sown. But nature had another card to play — it would freeze earlier this year than any other year in the memory of earlier settlers. The wind turned from the north, and the temperature drop astonished the settlers. In their experience in Canada, nothing had matched this weather pattern. From a warm and balmy afternoon with all the prospects of a delightful fall evening, came a breath of cold, like a stab of pain, alerting both Nick and Erena that there was trouble ahead. Erena expressed her concern for the garden and Nick echoed with his concern for the wheat.

"Erena," Nick suddenly called, "let's collect some dry branches and build little fire pots in your garden. We'll light them and save some of your more delicate garden plants."

"That's a good plan. The peas and beans are just starting to fill and maybe your idea may save them," Erena answered.

They went out together and collected firewood and made four small piles upwind from the plants, leaving them there to light when the frost would come. After midnight, Nick got up from their bed and lit the fires. Around daybreak, Erena threw more wood on the embers. The temperature had reached the freezing point.

They learned that their Eden carried an evil breath. The frost browned the vegetation in the garden and curled the leaves of the wheat, but the plants near the fires did not suffer at all. Many of the early plants that provided fruits and vegetables from above ground had already ripened, been picked, stored, or consumed, while those below ground would mature smaller but remain edible.

The wheat, however, would suffer. The kernels would ripen prematurely. It would make flour, but germination could be affected. Nick was disillusioned. He would have to cut the grain early, and collect, dry, thresh, and store it. Before planting next spring, he would count out a hundred random kernels and plant them in soil in the shack. The number that sprouted would give him an idea of how the frost had affected germination.

Nick only allowed his disillusionment to trouble him briefly. He reflected that the grain showed so much promise. "It will be better next year; meanwhile, there is going to be wheat for flour. We won't starve this winter, or ever again," he rationalized.

Over the summer months, Nick broke more land, and in the spring he planned to sow the new land to oats, some for their animals and fowl and some for oatmeal for the family. "A year from now we will be selling grain," he informed Erena. She, in turn, assured him there would be garden produce to sell this fall. The garden was producing substantially more than the three of them could use during the winter. The one night frost was unfortunate but not disastrous.

Wild plants were an early source of fruit. Saskatoon berries, raspberries, and strawberries ripened, and were picked and preserved. The wild strawberries were so succulent that even George would stoop down and pick them alongside the path to the river. Wild currents and cranberries withstood the frost, and these were harvested into late fall.

Erena developed a lifelong appreciation for nature's gift in the natural food it offered. She picked the berries, carefully stepping around the mother plants to avoid any injury to *God's gifts*, as she called them. Not a berry would be wasted. After picking, they were canned or eaten, and there were pails of them. The excess garden produce was sold to workers that were clearing the right-of-way for the railroad. The money was used to buy canning supplies.

They plastered the outside of the house and barn while the weather was warm. Nick converted one of the extra stalls in the barn for a chicken house and installed two laying boxes for the hens.

Within the first year on the homestead, they had a shack, a small granary, and a substantial barn that yet needed a loft and a tin roof. The progress was remarkable because, beyond these physical structures, there was an ample food supply, a cow, and wheat enough to grind to provide all the baking flour they would need. The Lazoruk families equaled the Woronuk development, but Steve Chalus had more land under cultivation, a bigger barn, and a larger granary. Besides, Elana's garden was larger!

Far back in history, man had learned to grind grain into flour by first building a mortar and pestle. The system had been well known worldwide for thousands of years. It was to be the method that these settlers would use to make flour before they could afford to use flourmills.

Erena used a large wooden mortar and pestle, made by Yakiew while in Manitoba, to grind wheat and other grains for baking. She had brought her coffee grinder from Manitoba, and this served as a preliminary grind. The mortar and pestle then ground the grain into the fine flour she needed for baking. She used these devices throughout her life to break down special grains, like poppy seeds, when she needed to control grain particle size.

In late August, Nick sharpened his scythe and cut the wheat crop by hand. He and Erena tied the wheat into bundles and stooked them upright to complete the drying process. Then, with flails, they thrashed the wheat out of the bundles, and on a breezy day, separated the wheat from the chaff by throwing it into the air and letting the wind blow the light chaff away as the heavy wheat kernels fell to the ground. They harvested about forty bushels of wheat.

Nick took a handful of kernels and chewed them, resisting the urge to swallow until they formed a gum. From that he estimated the gluten content. His wheat was better than any other variety he had tested. Marquis was high in gluten, and Erena would make great bread from it. When they had a few free moments, Nick and Erena walked to the granary and just stood in the doorway admiring the little pile of wheat in the corner — their first year's crop.

When Nick had asked Erena to marry, love was just a potential sequel that could come from achieving goals together. Now, three years after, having suffered and succeeded together, a true and lasting love had developed. Two young people, burned by the sun, their hands like course leather, skin blotched from mosquito bites, could look into each other's eyes and find in them a depth of meaningfulness that would bind them together for the rest of their lives.

# CHAPTER 31

Letters from Nick and Mike to their relatives in Arbakka were rapidly creating enthusiasm to move to the Peace River country. In 1914 there was an exodus from Arbakka and adjacent impossible farming areas in Manitoba. The land farther north along the Spirit River was soon taken, and the homesteads to the east were being applied for. Nick Woronuk, Nick Lazoruk, Mike Lazoruk and Steve Chalus all had built the essential buildings: shacks for themselves, barns for the animals, and storage bins for produce.

The Fred Sandul family moved to the lands on which young Fred had filed homestead applications the previous year. The east side of the basically north flowing Spirit River was occupied largely by Austro-Ukrainians, and many who were interrelated by marriage. The area became a collection of Slavic people fostering a natural tendency to preserve customs and traditions that they had practiced in their mother country.

The families were young, more children were born, and the little trail leading to the Calkin-English General Store and the Revillion

Frères Fur Trading Store in Spirit River Settlement was travelled sufficiently that it might better now be termed a road. Rarely would a traveler pass without some expression of a greeting, or stopping for a conversation. Homesteading in remote areas had that characteristic. It was a lonely existence, and passersby were events to observe, welcomed to the homes, and always fed whatever fare was available.

There were positives to this stark environment: there was honesty, and respect for the bounty that came from one's struggles. No homes had locks, no thefts occurred, and a fellowship evolved between families and friends that was lasting. Home sites were selected as near to a water supply as possible, and, in that respect, they followed the meandering Spirit River. The trails and roads that connected these sites naturally followed a similar course. It represented a practical approach to building a rural community.

On the west side of the Spirit River lived Metis, English, French, and an occasional German family. The diversity on the west side did not lend itself as strongly to community spirit as occurred on the east side. There was a craving for a uniting facility for the Slavs to which each would sense a commitment.

Still devoted to their Orthodox faith, the Slavs' immediate need was a church and a cemetery. Tradition held that cemeteries and churches were on the same site, as they were in Bukovina. Further, the cemetery needed to be on a raised portion of land to protect it from flooding. Most importantly, there was the tradition: in burial, the head of the deceased was to be slightly higher than the feet. A slope provided that advantage. A church would be built at the pinnacle of the hill with an Orthodox cupola, representing its call to worship.

Mike and Nick Lazoruk were experienced in such construction. They had personally taken major roles in the construction of the first Ukrainian Greek Orthodox Church in Canada while living in Arbakka.

The four families searched for an appropriate site. It was Steve Chalus who had explored an area to the east of his land. It contained a unique knoll that rose gently thirty feet or so above the flat land around it. That seemed to him to be an excellent site for a cemetery and a church. The other families visited the area, walked the knoll, and agreed that this was to be the site where their deceased would be buried, and a church built. It would bind the living and the dead in their tradition each Sunday morning.

Following the successful application to reserve the site for a cemetery, an even more intense bustle of activity and camaraderie developed among the people of Orthodox faith. They were going to have the first symbol of their identity established amongst them. It was a peculiar reaction: on the one hand it would serve to fill the needs of worship, while on the other hand, it was a clear attempt to segregate themselves from the neighbors who defined them as indifferent to the support of the British.

But there were other problems to contend with. In contrast to Bukovina, there were no priests in the area, and among the settlers there were Greek Orthodox and Greek Catholic adherents. The Greek Catholic contingent, mixed with Roman Catholicism from Polish influence and occupation, had emigrated mostly from Galicia, or Halychyna as it was referred to in the local vernacular. In Manitoba, where they had first settled, Catholic and Orthodox had intermarried and some of their children were still unbaptized, waiting for a priest to carry out the ritual.

In the minds of the four families, there was a significant difference between Orthodoxy and Catholicism. Their religious teachings did not dwell on the similarities, the original roots, or common purpose that should have encouraged mutual respect. Instead, their understanding was that an irreconcilable difference separated them. The cemetery needed to be for those of Orthodox faith exclusively.

Nick Woronuk spoke of the conundrum: "The children play together, grow together, marry, and there is no issue to prevent them from living a normal life. It is at death that ugly religious ideologies separate them." He knew the practice was wrong, but he found that he was powerless to change it. Initially, the Greenway Cemetery was a site for the Greek Orthodox Church and a burial ground for adherents to that faith. This issue was another stab into a sensitive relationship that was developing in the rural community around the church and the cemetery.

The factors that caused a separation between the Galicians and the Bukovinians was not religion alone; there was, as well, a historic perspective. Galicia carried with it not just the symbol of being Catholic, but the history of the callous atrocities that were perpetrated on Ukrainian people in that northern province during its occupation by Poland. These would not be forgotten. The Orthodox faith, without serious study, resembled Greek Catholic that, in turn, differed only moderately from Roman Catholic. Yet here, thousands of miles from where the issues originated, in an isolated little settlement where every passing neighbor stopped to visit, it would surface to strain in death the unique relationship that the settlers enjoyed in life.

It took over a year before title was obtained to the ten-acre plot that would be named *Greenway Cemetery*. It would become the final resting place for all these settlers, when their time came, and entomb with them the litany of hardships, tragedies, successes, and joys into this, their final resting place.

# CHAPTER 32

During the summer of 1914, Dad again walked the Edson Trail to guide my grandfather, George, back to the homestead. (George and the rest of the family had returned to Canada in 1910.) Now familiar with the terrain and the vicissitudes of weather in the foothills of the Rocky Mountains, Dad was better prepared. What he did not realize was that his father's health had deteriorated since they had last seen each other. The return walk for grandfather was difficult, and Dad had to pay to have George ride with a settler who was making the trip to the Peace River country. Dad walked the trail in order to save money.

The little shack now housed Nick, Erena, their son George, and the elderly George Woronuk. It was crowded, but it was home. Even with weakening health, George began clearing his homestead to satisfy the requirements of the Dominion Lands Act. Eventually George exchanged that quarter section for more suitable land to the south. This turned out to be fortuitous, for in later years, the town of Rycroft developed on this site.

George Woronuk was a pipe smoker. Not an occasional smoker, but a persistent one, resting the pipe's stem on the left side of his mouth, even when it was not lit. It was a curved pipe with the bowl top below the level of his lower lip. It had accumulated the aromas of old tobacco such that if he misplaced it, Erena could locate it by the odor it emanated. He used plug tobacco because it was the least expensive, and he whittled flakes from it with great care in order to not waste a gram, carefully arranging them into the bowl and then compressing them with his index finger. It was more than a necessary routine; it was ritual.

Whether in the heat of summer, with mosquitoes having a feeding frenzy on his bare hand, or during the vicious cold of winter, with his fingers immobile from the cold, George took time to fill and light his pipe in precisely the same manner. Even his son Nick, who had never smoked a day in his life, would pause to see the process carried out, methodically and precisely, as though it sanctioned a critical passage into some exotic environment.

Once lit, followed by some quick inhalations to ignite the contents, George's shoulders would straighten as though the smoke provided analgesics to a chronic pain, and an expression of contentment would spread across his features. George was addicted to his pipe, the instrument that would take his life.

He was a gentle man. Anger was foreign to him, and in his entire adult life he never once expressed it openly to others around him. He was the same with pain. With no dental care, his teeth and the tissues that supported them had become diseased, and he must have suffered intense pain from this condition. He extracted his back teeth with common pliers and never murmured a word regarding the agony of his own making.

The crusty weeping lesion on his lower lip, precisely where the stem of his pipe rested, was growing, and it extended slowly into the deeper tissues of the lip. The pain must have been severe, but George never complained, nor did he quit smoking or even change the position of his pipe. He was that type of man. Deeply dedicated to his children and to the wife he had lost, he did not remarry nor did he ever show the slightest interest in that matter. He chose to live with his son, or with his daughter Sophia (affectionately called Zoyka or Zoya), and provide what service his failing body could, to the family he lived with.

Sophia had married in Manitoba to a giant of a man, by comparison to those of Slavic descent in the area. His name was George Rosko; he stood well over six feet tall and weighed easily 250 lbs. He was deployed frequently as a settler of disputes, and his size and strength were respected, if not dreaded. Sophia was stunningly attractive and personable.

They too left Manitoba in 1913, but moved to Radway, Alberta, the area that Nick Woronuk and Mike Lazoruk had considered, but had found the forest growth too dense to convert to a successful farm operation. Nick's letters to his sister Sophia expressed the soil quality and potential of the Spirit River Settlement. Sophia persuaded George to abandon his homestead in Radway and join her family and his sister Domka in the Peace River country.

In 1915, George and Sophia packed their meager belongings and travelled to Edmonton. By this time, the British Columbia and Edmonton Dunvegan (B.C.&E.D) railroad had reached McLennan, Alberta, about 90 miles from the Spirit River Settlement. Sophia and George, with two daughters, arrived at this location in the spring of 1915. Nick was waiting there to meet them. He had taken his oxen team to help move the Rosko family to his home.

The shack that Nick had built two years earlier now served, for a brief period, a house for eight people, five adults and three children. By now, Erena had whitewashed the walls and plastered the outside. Much of the moisture had evaporated from the green logs, and the dwelling, although small, was comfortable. The floor was still of dirt but covered in plaster, dried and hardened to a state resembling ceramic tile, functioning as well as any constructed from wood. It seemed to absorb heat from the stove/heater, and even during the winter cold, it was warm. Erena could wash it and sweep it like a conventional floor, and children could play on it throughout the year without having to wear footwear. With his father's help, Nick built another room to the shack, and installed another heater to make the space comfortable and to dry the logs. This second room acted as a bedroom for the family and guests while children slept in the main part. The shack now became a house. It was a visible step forward in prosperity and an improved quality of life.

The tilled acreage had multiplied, and in 1915 frost was not a problem. It yielded a bumper crop. They had more than they could thrash by hand and needed advanced machinery to do the task. They hired a threshing machine and crew, shared between the four families, then hauled wagon loads of grain to McLennan and made the first tangible money from their farming operations. The railroad was destined to reach them by next year.

Erena's surviving chicks, three hens and two roosters, grew to become full-grown chickens. In the spring of 1915, she had saved enough eggs to have two brood hens set and in three weeks she had nearly twenty chicks. Nick's little wire enclosure for the fowl was too small so he built two more. Erena could now separate the broods with their hens. With his .22 rifle, Nick had reduced the number of hawks by occasionally eliminating one that ventured too close. The remainder became wary, and although they made their regular visits, they were not a threat to the broods in the enclosures.

Early one spring morning in 1915, around daylight, the silence was broken by a cacophony of squawking hens. The hen enclosure was near the house and the adults were awakened by the panic in the yard. Nick looked out the window just in time to see a grey animal disappearing under the granary he had built.

When he went out to investigate he found one rooster missing, and a blanket of feathers where the kill had been made. He found a thin long pole with which he could reach under the granary and dislodge whatever animal had made the kill. As he poked randomly around, he suddenly struck something flesh-like and received, in return, a vicious snarl. He continued to poke, more vigorously now that he had it isolated, and finally, with a sudden thrashing of feet, the beast left its quarters and exited but twenty feet from him. Snarling and spitting, its tufted ears turned back and eyes glaring at Nick, it crouched in a position ready to spring at him. It was a full-grown lynx — and it was not backing away. Nick's only protection was the pole he was holding; it offered no protection against a wild cat.

Nick motioned to Erena, standing near the door of the house, to bring the gun. She quickly re-entered the house; Nick and the lynx stood motionless staring each other down. Erena loaded the gun as she cautiously approached Nick from behind. She slipped the gun into his right hand and she too stood motionless as Nick slowly raised it to his shoulder. There was the sharp crack of the bullet exploding; the lynx spun, sprang two uncoordinated leaps toward the bank of the river — and collapsed.

Nick skinned the lynx and stretched the hide, fur side down, on a plank much as he had seen done in the trapper's cabin on the Edson Trail. "Who knows," he told Erena, "the Hudson's Bay store may give me a dollar for putting my life on the line. I should get enough," he quipped, "to pay for the rooster and the shell."

"You and money," Erena teased, "you keep the money, but I want my rooster back."

Nature seems to signal its wild inhabitants when dinner is ready. Yes, the lynx paid with its life, but in so doing, it seemed to alert a variety of equally noxious chicken loving predators to haunt the chicks and the grown hens. The telltale odor of a skunk, the dead chicken with puncture wounds to the neck — the works of a weasel — and the late evening and early morning hoots of owls now added to Erena's concern for her brood. There were losses, to be sure, but the setting hens stayed ahead of the disasters, and by fall, Erena had several dozen chickens, and Nick had built a log henhouse for their comfort and safety. It was war! Similar forts were established at the two Lazoruk and the Steve Chalus farms.

For all his skill as a driver of oxen and horses, Nick Lazoruk was a disaster with a rifle. His quiescent nature may have had something to do with this trait. He detested killing or injuring anything, and when the marauders became intolerable to Maria, Nick invited his sniping brother-in-law to come and help out. Having learned in his own yard that patience is a feature essential to a hunter, he would sit motionless, early in the morning or into the evening hours, when the culprits would come out to feed on Maria's chickens, holding his little rifle loosely at his shoulder. He helped reduce their numbers, but as he so often said, "For every one I kill, the bitch will have given birth to two more."

During the winter months, a new sound pierced the frosty air and would wake the sleeping settlers. Coyotes had found the scent of domestic fowl irresistible, and were circling the farmsteads alerting each other with their whines and barks. When left undisturbed, they would progressively reduce the circle size, as if tightening a noose. Nick sometimes arose at night to shout at them, and they would become mute, but in a few minutes, their howls would begin again, as they closed in to where they were circling the pen itself.

In the early spring, yet another chorus entered nature's opera: it was a long high-pitched wail, with the addition of a vibrato as the note reached its duration — timber wolves! These choristers struck fear in the residents. They knew that in Eastern Europe wolves were known to kill people. Neither Nick nor Erena would ever see one, but their howl would be heard for many years, always distant: a reminder that the wolves knew where the settlers were, but the settlers did not know where the wolves were. The advantage was clearly in favor of the wolves.

Erena carried George in her arms as she walked to visit her sister Elana one winter's day. On one such trip, she saw dog-like tracks — but much larger — in the fresh snow. She knew these were the tracks of the wolves; she had heard them howling the night before. They were midway between the Chalus's and her own home. Shivers went up her spine; they were there, probably watching her and George. A few steps farther she could see the remains of a deer they had killed and devoured. Panic began to grip her. She clutched her son tight to her body and ran the rest of the way. Erena showed such fear that Steve harnessed his horses, hitched them to a sleigh, and drove mother and child home when the visit was over.

During the winter of 1915-16, Nick worked for the Edmonton-Dunvegan and British Columbia Railroad helping build the bed for the coming rail. It was menial work, pushing a wheelbarrow filled with gravel and dumping it to level the bed for laying the tracks. There were probably twenty-five men similarly employed, and almost all were new settlers on land between McLennan and the Spirit River Settlement.

Everyone needed cash and there were only two sources: work on the railroad or bootleg liquor. Nick did both.

He set up a still. A large tree had fallen over near the river's edge. Its surface was to form a hidden pathway branching off the main trail to the river. By walking on this downed tree, no tracks were visible into the bush: an ideal site, he thought.

By now Erena's gardens were producing surplus potatoes, and she picked wild raspberries, currants, and saskatoon berries, some of which she preserved for food, and some which would be mashed for producing spirits. Each of these plants had the sugar and starch contents that made them suitable for converting to ethanol, a consumable alcohol.

The political situation at the time was responding to the American influence that had adopted prohibition of alcohol consumption. It wasn't working in the United States and had brought on one of the most barbarous of all crime waves in that nation. Yet, pressured by women's organizations in Canada, the Federal Government dumped the responsibility onto the Provincial Governments. By 1915, it seemed clear that Alberta would be adopting prohibition soon.

In the Spirit River area, like elsewhere in the country, the native population craved the euphoria that alcohol created. They had little use for the money that the government provided as a monthly stipend; they were anxious to trade money for alcohol. But money was a critical ingredient for the settler to buy the materials necessary for the growth of his enterprises. The conditions were optimum for the barter of liquor for money, in contradiction to the evolving laws of the land.

Settlers made a home-brew that contained various levels of alcohol, and some carelessly included alcohols that were toxic. The natives quickly recognized good sources and those that were dangerous. Nick and Erena were reputed as a good source, using techniques that they brought with them from Bukovina to Manitoba and now to Alberta.

They knew that the first part of the initial condensation could contain toxins, and it had to be discarded. Later in the boiling of the brew, the ethanol evaporated, then condensed in the winter cold, and this product they collected. Next they redistilled it and evaporated more water, ending with more concentrated liquor. It was a lengthy process, carried out mostly at night, in cold weather, when the outside temperature was such that it would cool the vapors and condense them.

The law against selling liquor to natives was well known, but survival demanded cash and the natives had cash. Bootlegging was a mechanism for accessing that essential commodity.

But with every such source there were drawbacks. The natives easily became addicted to liquor and posed what the settlers perceived as a threat. Their demand was insatiable, and those that provided the *fire-water*, as they referred to it, would be constantly intruded upon to provide more. Mike Lazoruk learned this early in his hay purchase; the hay was a savior for his animals, but he was, thereafter, frequently hassled to barter for more liquor.

The second issue was the law itself. Police might find the still and arrest the bootleggers. That would involve either significant fines, or internment, or both. At the time, settlers had not yet learned to trust the natives with keeping the source of their liquor supply secret and dealt cautiously with them. They learned, much later, that natives rarely divulged information, and they could have been trusted unreservedly. The gangs of workers on the railroad were, seemingly, a better source of extra income. Nick Woronuk, working with them, offered his homebrew at a nominal price.

The word eventually got to the police that one source of liquor was likely the Woronuk farm. One wintry day, a police officer of the Royal Northwest Mounted Police, as the force was named at the time, rode up on his horse to inspect the premises, on the grounds that he had knowledge that a still operated on the Woronuk property. He circled the periphery of the cleared home site, not venturing into the river area.

It was an interesting, albeit frightening, experience. Did he clearly not want to find the still? He knew, as everyone did, that bootlegging was the only source of income for the destitute settler. Take away this one source and the settler could starve. The small amount of liquor that was produced was insignificant, but it provided just enough cash income to supply the struggling settlers with some purchasing power. Erena and Nick had stashed the flasks of moonshine in the snow along the path from the house to the barn, thus avoiding leaving tracks in the snow to more likely hiding places. The constable rode his horse over the path several times but failed, or chose not to notice the containers hidden beneath the snow. When he was through, he came to report that he did not find any sign of illegal liquor on the premises. Erena offered him lunch and a chance to warm himself in the house. He accepted.

# CHAPTER 33

In January of 1916 Erena gave birth to her second son, whom they named William. Even at birth, William was a strong, well-proportioned infant. Nick Woronuk was overjoyed to have two sons. With the extra money Nick earned working on the railroad bed, he was able to buy a second cow. Now Erena had sufficient milk available to feed her two children year-round at home. The farm operation was obviously moving into a viable business. Erena had over fifty chickens, as well as some ducks and geese, and Nick's sniper shooting had lowered the predator population to where the fowl were able to range around the yard in relative safety.

Growth was apparent in each of the four farm operations. Steve Chalus, whose physical labors were the envy of all, continued to drive himself mercilessly and cleared more land than the others. Each had cleared significantly more than the minimum requirement for maintaining their homesteads. They marveled at the amount of land to which they would soon gain full title. It was a joyous time in each of the four households.

However, the issue of discrimination still remained. As World War I dragged on, it became obvious that this was not going to be a brief skirmish that had influenced the young British men to join the army. By 1916, Canadian infantry had already distinguished itself in several battles in France, particularly in the Second Battle of Ypres. News of this success only heightened the level of discrimination against Austrians like the Woronuk, Lazoruk, and Chalus families. Erena was finding it difficult to cope with meeting anyone of Anglo-Saxon heritage. Although she understood little English, it was not difficult to see the distaste her presence created in any association with them.

Progressively, she and the other Slavic women withdrew from any social interaction with the *English* that would have helped them develop a working knowledge of the English language. The Spirit River Settlement fractured into two camps as a result of such prejudice: those whose first language was English and those whose first language was not. It was to remain that way for years.

The long-promised railway arrived in the summer of 1916. It was a joyful sound when the first steam engine blew its whistle, belched its steam, and squealed to a halt near the Spirit River Settlement.

Nick Woronuk continued to work the winter months on the railway construction gangs, and his English improved. He now chose to learn to read and write in English; until then he had been limited to signing his name. He subscribed to the Western Producer newspaper; it was the most popular agricultural newspaper since its inception in 1913. His background in German helped immensely. The Latin alphabet was already familiar to him, and the large number of similarities between the two languages served as a foundation to understanding the written English text.

He applied himself to this task assiduously, and in a few months, he was able to read with some understanding the only English text they had in the house. He anxiously awaited the arrival of each issue and was waiting at the post office in Doc Calkin's store often before the mail was sorted. Not only was he reading but he was learning. The Western Producer was dedicated to information for farmers, and from his readings he was able to pass valuable knowledge to his neighbors.

The farming and ranching community anxiously waited for the trains to come in order to have a convenient mechanism to ship their produce to markets around the world. Carloads of material goods began to flow in, and carloads of raw products began to flow out. Lower freight rates offered opportunities to buy products at less cost. Doc Calkin's little store was quickly overwhelmed with merchandise.

Doc decided to move his store closer to the railway station that was built approximately two miles east of the Spirit River Settlement site. It was becoming clear that the hamlet of Spirit River was in a name conflict with the Spirit River Settlement. A new name would have to be assigned to the businesses collecting near the railway station.

The ED&BC rail provided passenger cars so that passengers were able to travel in comfort to the new settlements in the northwestern part of Alberta. Word had come from Edmonton that a Greek Orthodox priest was preparing to visit the community. The excitement for most of the residents was overwhelming, but Nick Woronuk and Mike Lazoruk, having already experienced the wrath of the church ministry, viewed the occasion with some skepticism. Their major objection was that the church waited until rail travel made the trip comfortable, yet damned them while they made the journey by the Edson Trail. But they were still Orthodox, albeit wary ones.

A priest did come, and the women expressed their strong faith by washing the priest's feet, mimicking an episode following Christ's washing of the feet of His disciples, described in the Bible. It was the highest expression of esteem they knew how to show, and the priest accepted the old country tradition with a degree of ostentation. He was provided with the finest meals and the best bed in each house he visited, and he discussed the plans for a church to be built on the cemetery site that would soon be registered as the Greek Orthodox Greenway Cemetery.

At the Woronuk home, he baptized little William using the kitchen table as an altar, and Spirit River water, which he blessed with reference to the Jordan River. In his prayers on behalf of the child, he prayed that William would grow under the influence of Christian fellowship. Nick listened carefully, the ritual essentially the same as he had heard numerous times in Onut and in Arbakka. It was ritualistic, but it was profound, and it brought back many of the sensuous feelings about Orthodoxy by which he had been raised, tempered only by the confrontation at the railway yards in Vita.

Erena had been preparing all day, and had sacrificed one of her precious geese, cooking it in cream, according to a recipe that she had long ago learned from her mother. Nick and Maria Lazoruk and George and Zoya Rosko were asked to stand as godparents, and according to Orthodox ritual, it was they who held little William while the priest baptized him. The four Nick Lazoruk children were present, and the little shack was crowded for this important ceremony. The conversation around the table ceased as the priest blessed the food and all those present. His demeanor was one of sincerity and depth of purpose, and the children seemed mesmerized by the man. It was then that he chose to relate his concern.

"How is it," he chided as his eyes met each of the adults at the table, "that you, who purport to be Orthodox, allow your children to play with Catholic children?"

There was a complete hush around the table. Not one spoon clicked on the dishes; not one jaw closed on the food already in the mouth.

Erena stopped on her way carrying a dish of extra food to the table. The silence lasted several long seconds and then Nick Woronuk spoke:

"Pastor," he began, slowly but emphatically, enunciating every word with clarity in order that it was understood by all, "with the children here I cannot say what I have in my heart, but when they have departed, I shall, I promise you, Pastor, set you and the church to which I *belonged*, straight. You, Pastor, have touched on a subject that I will not condone. We, who live here, are Christians of a faith you clearly do not understand. But tonight, you will."

It took some time before normal conversation resumed. The pastor had lost his appetite, and it was only after Erena pleaded with each person at the table to eat more, that some degree of normality began to return. The pastor remained red-faced, tried to overcome his embarrassment by first resorting to questionable humor, and finally chose to revert back to pomposity. Neither worked in his favor, and he must have felt that he was misplaced in this midst.

When the other guests rose to leave the table and began to prepare to leave the house, the pastor made some effort to go with them and save further embarrassment. George Woronuk, feeble and emaciated, led his son to one side and whispered, "Let it be, Nicholai; he is not God, but a mortal like you and I." He paused, looked into his son's eyes, and added, "We all feel like you do, but only you have the will to correct this man. Choose your words carefully, because I know you will confront him. Leave us a place for eternal rest."

It was a touching statement from a wise man. It was true, Nick would confront the pastor, and it is possible that the gentle words of his father may have defused the tone Nick might have chosen. George put his hand on his son's shoulder and looked into Nick's blue eyes, then removed his hand and set his son free. Nick stood there for a moment, allowing his father's words to penetrate, then turned to walk to the pastor.

"Pastor," he said, slowly leading the man away from the women helping Erena with food and dishes, "what I have to say may take a while. I ask you not to interrupt me, because the words I will use are not those that my lips want to utter; these will be the words from my heart." Nick took a breath, paused a second or two and continued:

"First, let me thank you for bestowing the wonders of baptism upon my son William, in such traditional and professional manner in our humble home. I will now pay you for your service, the exact amount that you had quoted me earlier today. Nick was holding the $2.00 in his hand and passed it to the pastor. Then he continued: "You have travelled a long way by train to reach this settlement. We came by oxen, as did the English, French, German, and others who may have preceded or followed us before the rail arrived, and we all suffered untold anguish. Our wives have honored you like no other man in their lives; they have washed your feet as an expression of their faith, in the belief that you, by your office, carry to them the word of God."

By now Nick Lazoruk, George Rosko and George Woronuk stood within hearing distance and one by one the women began to gather next to them and listen. The children played with each other some distance away, chasing and laughing, unconcerned by the silence around them. Nick continued:

"And I, too, anxiously waited for your arrival to restore my faith. Yes, my faith, because my life and that of my wife and first child was made possible in this environment by the cooperation of my neighbors alone. You see, the Metis who provided us with eggs to raise the fowl that we now have, and served to you — are Catholic. The Metis that sold me the cow that produced the milk that was on our table and may have saved the life of my son — he, too, is Catholic. The owners of the store that extended credit to me when I had no cash remaining, neither their religion nor mine was ever an issue. When I needed work on the railroad, my religion was never questioned, and my pay was the same as every other man of faith or without it. Yes, I, and those you see standing around us, are suffering prejudice because our homeland is the enemy in a useless war, but adding to it are our customs and our religion. We have made some moves to integrate, and maybe when this conflict is over, we may be comfortable among all our neighbors. But our children play together, and depend on each other for the comfort that children find in their play. They share their company, their food, and their toys without questioning whether they are Catholic, or Orthodox, or any other faith. And so we have lived for the past three years with hope and anticipation that we will all prosper by our individual efforts, and those that living with neighbors provides.

The pastor shuffled, coughed a little, continued to stare at his shoes but remained silent. Nick went on:

"At dinner you asked us why our children played with Catholic children. Your words and their inflection suggested that mode was not in keeping with our Orthodox faith. You come here with education, you have attended Seminary, you are an ordained priest; we are none of those. But when we needed your comforting words on the trail, or living in a cave that first winter, you were not with us. We used our own ingenuity to survive, and we prayed, without ritual, just prayed, and not just for ourselves, but also for the Catholics, or for any other human beings who might have benefited from our prayers. Your suggestion at the table ignores all this. It implies we are at fault. We should not associate with other faiths. To me, that was, is, and always will be impossible. At this moment, I no longer respect you as a pastor of my faith. I accept you as an ordinary man, and I offer to you the same offerings

I would to any other ordinary man who comes to my door. I will not again attend an Orthodox service except for baptism and death."

The pastor stood stunned. For the next few moments he remained silent. Then he raised his head, stood erect, and as though he had not heard a word, he turned to the adults around him and blessed them with the sweep of his arms, outstretched, such that the blessing included Nick. It was a remarkable response under pressure. In his blessing he thanked Erena and the women for making him so welcome; he thanked the Lord for providing Nick and Erena with another son, and then he thanked Nick for the words, pausing momentarily, "...that Seminary never taught."

George was rightfully proud of his son. He placed his hand on Nick's shoulder for a second time, looked at him, and did not have to say a word. Erena, too, squeezed her husband's hand and, when free of the other women, asked how he could have spoken such words in such a short time. Nick answered simply, "They were not my words. They were words that came through me."

Nick later spoke of the experience with the pastor to Mike Lazoruk and Steve Chalus and admitted to them that his words flowed from him with uncharacteristic fluency. He was, in his own right, a charismatic speaker, but this dialogue may have exceeded what was natural to him. He never regretted his stand, and thereafter lost most interest in religious matters.

However, he was keenly involved in the assignment of the ten-acre plot for the cemetery. His father was failing rapidly, and Nick knew that it would not be long before his father passed. The cancer on his lip was spreading to portions of his lower face and neck; it was just a matter of time before a vital organ would be invaded and his father's life would end.

Old George Woronuk was living with his daughter Zoya, but as the disease progressed, he asked that he live out the rest of his days with his son. Erena then provided him with the best care she was able to, for she adored Nicholas's father, his gentleness and kindness.

The little log church with an Orthodox cupola was carefully constructed by the group and was nearly finished when George Woronuk passed away on January 21, 1918. He was the first adult buried in the cemetery, which his favorite son had played a major role in selecting.

# CHAPTER 34

1 916 drifted into 1917, and as the year progressed, news of a deadly flu epidemic reached the settlement. At first, it was supposedly confined to Spain and was incorrectly referred to as Spanish flu. Because Spain was not involved in WWI, the country's news was not subject to censorship, and mortality was honestly reported. The facts, later borne out, were that other European countries were more severely affected than Spain. In fact, theories abound that the extreme death toll from the flu may have turned the course of the war. German and Austrian soldiers were dying at rates that the war itself had never attained.

The highly contagious virus, already present in the United States and Canada, would soon spread its ravages to the Spirit River area as well. It made its appearance in the Spirit River Settlement in the native population early in 1918. Soldiers coming home from their rotations in Europe were sometimes quarantined in railroad stations, able to see their loved ones at a distance but not permitted to come into physical contact with them. The fear of contracting this deadly disease pervaded all settlements, and only a rare home survived without being ravaged by this killer.

The uniqueness of this disease was that it attacked the healthiest: those between 20 and 40 years of age. Their active immune systems over reacted to the virus. That brought on a violent pneumonia and caused the victims to die, drowning in their own phlegm. Pregnant women rarely survived. They aborted and progressed downwards, and in the course of a few days, they died.

Erena contracted the Spanish Flu. She might have been pregnant at the time, for she remembered bleeding with her toilet, and then the symptoms increased in violence, and she understood that death was imminent. Her major concern was the welfare of her two children, so she asked that Nick bring over Zoya Rosko, Nick's sister, to whom she would express her wishes. Nick, now owning a team of horses, drove to the Rosko homestead and asked his sister to come to speak to his dying Erena.

It was an emotional time. Nick and Zoya and even the powerful George Rosko wept, but Zoya came with Nick to see her sister-in-law. She stood in the doorway to the bedroom addition to maintain a safe distance from the contagion. Erena was in the grip of pneumonia, her chest so swollen that the surface tissues seemed ready to burst. In short breaths, she asked Zoya to take William as her son and leave George for Nick to care for. Zoya promised she would, as she had no sons and she was a godparent to William.

But Zoya was not one to succumb to the inevitable without battle. She immediately prepared a poultice of milk, mustard, garlic, and liniment, and had Nick apply this to Erena's chest to *draw-out*, as she described it, the offending disease. Nick had been attending to Erena and seemed immune to the virus. He spread the poultice over her chest and back, covered her with quilts, and waited.

The hours ticked by and Erena burned under the poultice, but persevered. By nightfall she was still alive and signs of ease of breathing seemed apparent. Through the night she suffered exacerbations of sweats and chills, at times burning with fever and at others unable to stay warm. But the chest began returning to normal and her breathing was improving. By morning, she was clearly healthier and was ravenously hungry. The tissues in her mouth had been bleeding, a sign of an advanced stage of the Spanish flu, chewing was painful, and the taste was altered. Though she craved food, she was able to consume only tiny portions.

Each day thereafter Erena improved. Word had spread about how ill she was, and how Zoya may have found a means of reversing the progress of the disease. Her poultice was regarded as a salvation, and the demand for its ingredients induced even the most prejudiced to knock on the door — for garlic — garlic at any price; the odor, the distinguishing feature of Slavism, notwithstanding. Garlic was believed to have healing properties; Nick and a weak Erena gave it out freely to whoever requested it. Their generosity would impress the frightened that came begging to their door. It's unknown if any lives were saved, but among the English-speaking residents of the area, there was a conspicuous reduction in the discrimination that was unleashed at the Austro-Ukrainians.

Whether it was from the ravages of the epidemic or bilateral fatigue, the war ended as suddenly as it had started. On November 11, 1918, an official armistice was signed, and four years of human savagery ceased. What was left of the Canadian contingent would soon return, some debilitated physically and mentally, but finally home.

They were heroes in the eyes of all Canadians, and even in the Spirit River Settlement, they were honored. The fact that most of them would have returned years earlier, had there been an option to do so, did not matter. Some had survived the gas attacks, their lungs permanently mutilated, unable to do a day's labor ever again, but that too was ignored. They were home, victorious and pompous. They had developed an intense hatred of the Hun, the German and Austrian enemy, whom they had fought for years in mud and trenches, and they would not soon forget. A return to their homeland was not a return to peace; it was into a battle not yet won. A new wave of discrimination faced the Austro-Ukrainians.

In contrast, the need for exportable produce was enormous. Grain prices were high. Now every farmer was producing substantial quantities of cereal grains for export, and the railway was capitalizing on its investment into the Peace River Country.

The Government of Canada offered homestead lands to veterans, and soon most unassigned land was granted to them. Many that chose to farm were unable to cope with the long hours of labor. Seeing the successful operation of the land by farmers of enemy descent only heightened their distaste for foreign interlopers. The bigotry became worse than the settlers had experienced previously, and even those who seemed tolerant in the past, now joined with the veterans in sneering and avoiding any relationship with the Ukrainian-speaking farmers. It was becoming intolerable.

In 1920, Nick Woronuk read an advertisement in the Western Producer that homestead land was being surveyed and made available to applicants in Jacksonville, Florida. The advertisements claimed excellent black loam land suitable for vegetable, fruit, and grain farming as well. The four families discussed the practicality of yet another move, thousands of miles away into the heat of a near tropical climate. The necessity to switch from grain to other agricultural products was discussed, but it would be in a foreign country where discrimination amongst those with white skin was unknown.

Erena, now fully recovered from her brush with death, said she feared the excessive heat, and that surely, with time, their contribution to nation building would overcome this narrow-mindedness. Her persuasive appeal helped turn the tide. They would attempt to tolerate the present condition, because it could not last.

Her judgment proved to be correct. Many veterans were unable to cope with the farming enterprise. Some soon became alcoholics, while others searched for business ventures in more actively growing communities, and others simply gave up farming and left the area.

A few remained, and they maintained a nucleus of intolerance, but over the years, as they aged and their memory of the war became secondary to their farming ventures, their tolerance of the settlers moderated. Occasional outbursts would occur, usually precipitated by alcohol, but these were rare and were accepted as part of the inevitable conditions of community growth.

In the year 1920, wheat prices reached an all-time high of $2.85 per bushel. Nick Woronuk had cleared and seeded the better part of a quarter section. He sold the wheat he raised and pocketed a handsome profit. Wheat prices would not hold, unfortunately, and by 1923 they had fallen to $1.00 per bushel, but most of the farmers were able to capitalize even when the prices were that low. The gardens continued to produce in excess, and Nick and the other members of the original Edson Trail group were living better than they had in all their previous years.

In 1920 Erena gave birth to her third son, whom they named Alexander. Alex, as he was soon to be called, made his presence known long before birth. Erena, laughing, talked about how he literally beat his way out of her abdomen. Neither of his older brothers so kicked nor fussed in utero, as did this boy. His life would center on this characteristic. His personality was as vivacious as his physical being, and he became the focal point of every gathering he attended.

George, his oldest brother, was now attending school, along with neighboring children. With scarcely a word of English in his vocabulary to start with, he excelled in all scholastic endeavors, and by the time he was through the first grade, he was as fluent in English as the children who were raised with English as their first language.

The evolution of spoken English within these families was interesting. The children who had learned the language in school communicated with each other entirely in that language. Communication with their parents continued to be in Ukrainian. George's brothers learned two languages from birth: Ukrainian from their parents and English from their older brother and neighboring children. In the first generation, all siblings were bilingual, some were able to communicate with children of other ethnic groups by learning Croatian or German, and a few developed a working knowledge of French. The common binding language was English, and it served to begin the long journey to ethnic acceptance.

The Spirit River Settlement had moved twice and was now being established at the site of the railway station. It was about then that a group of local businessmen are said to have entered their names into a hat and drew the name R. H. Rycroft, thereby naming the new site accordingly. Spirit River, as a community, developed six miles to the west. The confusion between Spirit River Settlement and Spirit River may have been solved by a name drawn from a hat.

# CHAPTER 35

T he end of the Great War brought on waves of nationalism among many peoples in Europe. The League of Nations struggled to satisfy the screaming hordes by defining new borders and new countries. Among these quests, were those made by Bukovinians and Galicians, desirous of an independent Ukraine. Ukrainian newspapers in Canada promoted this ideology, and it reached the little settlement of Austro-Ukrainians in Rycroft. The few families discussed this issue, and swayed by enthusiastic journalism and their own experience of being the enemy in the midst of the victors, they agreed that they were indeed Ukrainian Canadians and not Austrian. They dropped the Austro from the Austro-Ukrainian forever.

Ukraine did not achieve independence by a decision of the League of Nations. Bukovina became a part of Rumania and Galicia was absorbed by Poland. East of the Dnieper River, Russia absorbed the land and people into its communist experiment. An independent Ukraine did not exist, but in Rycroft, as in communities all across

263

Canada and the United States, a form of Ukrainian nationalism developed that excluded any name preceding Ukraine.

Frugal management of cash resources was an essential characteristic of successful settlers. The Ukrainian families that settled in Rycroft practiced it to the level of an economic science. Although having experienced survival without money a decade earlier, they knew the opportunities that cash resources could provide, and they shrewdly accumulated money with which they could improve their operation.

Nick Lazoruk and Nick Woronuk invested in a steam engine that was purported to be able to pull a load equal to the strength of twenty-five horses. The machine was cumbersome, inefficient, and required a steam engineer to run it. It needed a constant supply of water to maintain steam and an endless supply of firewood to keep the burner heating the water. Its value lay not in its mobility, but in a stationary position, where it could supply power that animals could not.

They bought a threshing machine and now were able to harvest their crops, and those of Mike Lazoruk and Steve Chalus as well. They purchased draft horses, strong, massive animals, with Belgian or Percheron blood, hoofs the size of kitchen plates, so many hands high that Nick Woronuk used a stepping stool to reach over their backs to harness them. The oxen, that had served them so diligently, were retired to the pasture, and their age soon claimed them.

Nick Woronuk rebuilt the barn he had hurriedly put together for the oxen. He added a few more logs to raise the wall height, and then built a gable roof covered with galvanized tin that would form a loft. The structure would last nearly a century. Nick and Mike Lazoruk built even bigger barns, and Steve Chalus outdid them all. The houses would have to wait. Human comfort was second to that of the animals and fowl.

The 1920s were an exciting time throughout North America and the excitement did not bypass Rycroft. Traditions were discarded like old socks, and a spirit of emancipation of women spread across the land like playing cards on a gambling table. Maria and Domka Lazoruk threw off their head covers, washed and cut their hair to a manageable length and, like Erena, bought sewing machines and Huron and McClary kitchen stoves with two baking ovens. White flour was purchased; feather-light white bread, raised to double the size of a loaf of bread from whole-wheat flour, graced their tables. The food of the gentry in Bukovina now was the food of the homestead farmer in Alberta.

Erena was surprised but elated when her fourth child, born in 1922, was yet another boy. They named him Meroslav, after a revolutionary of Ukrainian birth who had distinguished himself by fighting for the rights of peasantry in an abusive environment in Bukovina, then under Austria. The name was shortened to the beautiful name of Merose, and he too would distinguish himself in his lifetime. "Four sons but no daughters," Erena pined. One more try she would allow herself, and it surely would bring a daughter. Someday.

George continued to perform scholastically. William, who to his schoolmates and friends became Bill, had also begun school but with the advantage of a foundation in English. His physical body had the makings of a powerful young man with wrists already wider than his older brother's. His endurance was remarkable: he could bear the cold of winter with little cover, and amaze his mother by coming in out of the cold with a red face and bare hands showing no sign of the freezing temperature he had endured. Alex began to walk at eight months. The walk quickly turned to a run, and this pace was a characteristic he would have for all his youthful years. He was a living dynamo, with a personality to match.

Merose, as he grew from infancy to childhood, showed stunning attractiveness, with a black wavy head of hair that he inherited from his mother. Erena and Nick were justly proud of their four boys. Nick could see a future for each one of them as the farm operation expanded, but Erena could see education, education, and more education for her sons. The farm would have to wait because her boys would first be educated, and then take over the farm. They would have access to the very facet of life that she had missed.

In 1869, just two years after Canadian Confederation, a young man, Scottish by heritage and Irish by country of origin, whose name was Timothy Eaton, had opened a little haberdashery in Toronto. In 1912, Nick had purchased his violin at the family's sprawling Winnipeg store. The Eaton's catalogues were mailed to nearly every farm in western Canada, including those in Rycroft. In its heyday in the 1920s, Eaton's was the trendsetter, including offering material components for complete homes. It was a more defining institution than the maple leaf or the British Ensign. Its catalogue was said to be better read and more widely distributed in Canada than the Holy Bible. Each household was mailed two issues per year: a fall and winter, and a spring and summer edition. Scarcely a non-consumable purchase was made without consulting the Eaton's Catalogue. It remained so for half of the twentieth century, and it was a near national disaster when, through mismanagement and varying markets, it was forced into bankruptcy in 1999. It was through Eaton's mail-order purchases that the Woronuks, the Lazoruks, and the Chaluses raised their standard of living equal to the highest in the area. The prices were competitive or lower, and the quality was guaranteed or money refunded.

Eaton's may have done more to change the customs of recent immigrants than any other single factor. Smiling models wore clothing that suggested a progressive nation of trendy inhabitants. No matter how steeped were its readers in tradition and religion, the catalogue imprinted its influence.

The catalogue would sway the public away from Bohemian to North American customs and attire. Crinoline skirts, lipstick, bobby sox, leather shoes with bright metal buckles; Eaton's carried them all. Meticulous hairdos, men's hats, spats and suits; you just filled a simple order form and waited a week or two. Even in the one room school in Rycroft, the Eaton's catalogue was used to teach English to non-English speaking children by associating the picture with the name of the product. It brought an isolated area into the midst of society when the next train brought the goods. It was a marketing bonanza, and the T. Eaton family and its progeny managed it superbly for years.

Amusingly, the catalogue had yet to serve another usage:when the new issue arrived. The old dog-eared copy was relegated to the outdoor privy. There the lighter, softer pages were carefully torn free, hand wrinkled and ingloriously applied as necessary. The remainder acted as a reading diversion.

The log house enjoyed the material aspects of *The Catalogue*. Basic furniture was added: a couch, a manufactured table and chairs, and even a few superfluous items to decorate the interior. Four children in Canadian dress were indistinguishable from the other children with the exception of the language they spoke to their parents.

The parents were now Canadian citizens, although the country had not yet matured sufficiently to drop the yoke that linked all citizens to their heritage. Like all others who had immigrated to Canada, they were hyphenated English, French, Irish or, as in their case, Ukrainian-Canadians. It was not yet sufficient to use the term Canadian alone on any document that required a statement of citizenship; your heritage was required even for children born in Canada.

But the two room plastered log settler's house was crowded. There was money in the bank, horses in the barn, a small herd of cattle, some pigs and countless chickens, geese, and ducks, and a granary full of wheat. By all accounts, with the exception of the house itself, the operation was a successful agricultural establishment. Nick and Erena began to search out plans for a better house.

Aladdin Homes, a Michigan construction company, sent its catalogues to Canada and advertised that its precut lumber could be assembled into a home in a day. The prices were competitive with Eaton's, which also sold materials and plans, but the Aladdin concept appealed to Nick and Erena Woronuk. Throughout the mid-twenties they studied the catalogues diligently. They settled on a particular design that included a basement, a water cistern, and a substantial wood-burning furnace. Then Erena announced that she was to have yet another child. On November 18, 1928, a clear sunny day with the last of the threshing being completed, she gave birth. Attended to by her mother Wasylena, who had acted as midwife for the birth of each of the previous four children, Erena gave birth to yet another boy. Erena so wanted a daughter that her first impulse brought tears. Yet the tears were for a moment only, because Wasylena quickly reminded her that this was God's will and His judgment was not to be questioned. They would name him Yvon and that would be anglicized to John.

John's entry into the world was late, a space of more than six years between him and his older brother Merose. He would not enjoy the camaraderie of Merose and Alex, but he would find, a few years later, a great playmate next door, only a few months older, in Evelynne, the eleventh child in the Nick Lazoruk household.

Before John was born, his oldest brother had already left home to attend a higher level of education that was not yet offered in Rycroft. As a mere boy, George took the train to Edmonton and enrolled in a

Ukrainian boarding school where subjects were taught in English, but Ukrainian was used to sustain the language and preserve its culture. In that year, George learned the rudiments of reading musical score and began to learn to play the violin in a classical style. A Professor Darmont, whose skills as a violinist were locally respected, provided lessons. George excelled and soon became one of Darmont's favored students. In that year he had learned to read musical score and play well enough to participate in his school's Ukrainian orchestra. He was a consummate academic, responded well to the academic disciplines of the time, and brought home to his family his newfound skills as a violin player, already well above those of his father. He taught these skills to his younger brother Alex during the summer months when school was out.

Before the new Aladdin home was built in 1929, music was the key pastime of the family. Alex excelled much as his father had in Bukovina. His electric reactions, remarkable ear, and sense of rhythm soon superseded even that of his elder brother. Merose's skills developed too, though not at the pace of the prodigious Alex. Duets played by Alex and Merose became a family tradition, and when the house was built, Erena and Nick assigned one room to be the home's music room. Countless hours were spent there playing the duets of Pleyel, Mazas, and eventually Mozart and Beethoven. Each summer when George returned from Edmonton, he passed on his new techniques to his brothers. Both would become competent violinists, but Alex's skills remained the most remarkable.

Meanwhile Bill, whose musical ear was probably the most acute, expressed no interest in playing an instrument. His interest from childhood was directed to the science of farming. While his younger brothers participated in music, Bill thumbed through Eaton's catalogue visualizing how the equipment that was on the market could coordinate the power of several horses to pull heavier loads. His inter-est was so intense that Nick ordered a particular piece of equipment from Eaton's that would combine the load pulling capacity of several teams of horses. Bill's joy, when the order arrived, was overwhelming. It was clear that he was going to be a farmer.

John was but a year old when the family moved into the new Aladdin home. It was not built in a day as advertised, but a compe-tent English-trained carpenter and bricklayer named Archie Wherrell built it during the summer. Old country attention to detail, excellent fir and cedar wood, made this house so stable that it would last a century needing only superficial repair.

Nick and Erena had their new home completed in the last of the good years. The economies were suffering and the markets around the world were unstable. The great stock market crash occurred that fall, and the next decade would bring about another era of hardship to not just the settlers in question, but to the whole world.

The Great Depression, like the flu epidemic, affected every house-hold, some so severely that starvation and even death resulted from it in communities all over Canada. The source of money dried up, and within a year or two, Nick Woronuk, like all other farmers in the area, had to make major alterations in life style in order to survive.

Trying to break fresh land with the joint venture steam engine was no longer possible. The engine itself was rusting and becoming unus-able, and hiring an engineer to run it was economically impractical. Yet Nick, by hiring workers during the heady days of the late 1920's, had cleared substantial areas that were now ready for the breaking plow. Leaving the cleared land untilled was not an option. It would grow back to bush quickly, sprouting from the roots and seeds that remained in the ground.

By 1930, Bill, at fourteen years of age, was a competent farmhand. He had demonstrated his skill with power machinery on numerous occasions, and it was apparent to his dad that he could complement farming with horses by the use of a tractor. Even at this tender age, this youngster was powerful, and capable of handling horses without his father's assistance.

Machinery was selling cheaply because of the Depression, and they were able to buy their first piece of petroleum fueled power machinery, a 15-30 McCormick Deering tractor, and they bought a two-bottom breaking plow. Bill began his life as a farmer still in grade school, using every spare hour to break and till soil. In the summer months, George would come home to help on the farm, but he was clearly not made of the same *substance of the soil* as was his younger brother. His interest was entirely academic, and his skill with machinery or draft animals was limited. The focus for the grain farming operation was falling on Bill.

The Great Depression offered opportunity that at first seemed unlikely. Countless men rode the freight trains across the country looking for work at wages so low that even the destitute farmer could pay. Food was the important factor; these young men were starving. Some would volunteer to do any farm work for food and lodging alone. Erena's gardens produced abundant food that was no longer market-able, and by paying nominal wages and providing adequate food, the Woronuks were able to clear large swaths of land that Bill could break. In that sense, the Depression combined opportunity with disaster.

It was Nick's frugality and money management that identified opportunities during this critical period. Many farmers went bankrupt by their dependency on cash flow. Nick, a non-drinker, non-smoker, and non- gambler, coupled with a keen understanding of the value of even discarded material, always had a little cash to invest in the farm operation.

His lifelong optimism uplifted the family spirits as well as those of the other new settlers. Erena's generosity was an equivalent positive; no hungry man left her door unfed. And the door remained unlocked. Now she had five huge gardens that grew not only vegetables and berries for food, but also flowers for the spirit. Her garden was her Eden.

The mosquitoes that had so ravaged all living things two decades before were now tolerable pests. Smudges had to be built only when the humidity became high prior to rain. But there was a serious problem.

John, the youngest child, was ill. He seemed to be having constant abdominal pain, crying and doubling his knees under his chin. There was a physician in Spirit River, and he was asked to come to visit the sick child. The doctor was an older man with serious Parkinson's disease. It did not allow him to practice much more medicine than to provide pacification. His diagnosis was that John had a hernia, and that it would heal over time. He recommended the family be patient; the pain would go away.

His diagnosis was wrong. The condition was chronic appendicitis, and the patience that he recommended was leading to a catastrophe. By 1933, John, at the age of five, was no longer able to walk and cried constantly. Erena was desperate. She persuaded Nick to allow her to go to Grande Prairie to see another doctor. She spent some of the money they had saved to buy a train ticket. She carried her son to the hospital immediately but was refused entry until she paid a fee of $10.00 in advance. By now John was screaming uncontrollably, but the clerk would not relent. Desperate, Erena ran with her screaming child through the streets to the hotel where she knew Dora Lazoruk, her niece, was working. Dora had saved enough to lend Erena $10.00. She rushed back to the hospital and was allowed admittance. Dr. O'Brian had a quick look at the child and shouted for immediate help. The appendix had ruptured. The child was dying.

For two weeks following surgery, John was not expected to survive. Infection, fever, and a near starvation diet, as treatment dictated then, for an already emaciated boy, were factors that did not bode well for recovery. But the child did respond, and in three weeks, Erena was able to bring him home. Wasylena had come from the Lazoruk farm to stay for the sake of the children, and Domka, Maria, and Elana made regular trips to the Woronuk farm to give assistance. It was, again, a demonstration of interfamily cooperation that Erena and Nick would never forget.

The bill for the hospital stay and the medical expenses came in the mail. Nick did not have the money to pay the amount and decided to sell one of his cattle to raise at least some of that money. He took a fine steer to the railway and shipped it to Edmonton to an abattoir for slaughter. A week later he received a letter in the mail. Assuming it to be a cheque, he was stunned when it was a bill for two dollars. The animal had not brought sufficient funds to pay the freight!

Nick borrowed the necessary money from Steve Chalus, and to the absolute amazement of the hospital staff, in the heart of the Depression, he paid the full amount owing. It was the first time in his life he had to borrow money and it weighed on him heavily. He finally went to a bank in Spirit River where, based on his successful farm operation, he was able to arrange a loan, and he repaid his debts to Steve Chalus and to Dora Lazoruk.

At the end of every month, without fail, Nick either walked or drove his horse and buggy to Spirit River to make payments on the bank loan. His diligence and honesty impressed the banker and his status among the English improved. Repaying the debts that had been an embarrassment to Nick turned out to be a valuable attribute. He would later serve on several boards with grain companies and cooperative enterprises, based in part on his reputation with the bank.

His son John recovered from the major surgery and grew through the depression years to show academic interests. It remained Bill's responsibility to farm. He soon replaced his father as the operator on the land, using advanced machinery that augmented the land's production, and turned a profit.

# CHAPTER 36

T he silence that had initially typified the country, interrupted only by the howl of coyotes or the wail of wolves, was now transformed. The persistent sound of pistons from McCormick, Case, Hart Parr, and the wheeze of the one cylinder John Deere tractors, from daybreak to darkness, mixed with the occasional whinny of horses and the cackle of fowl, contrasted with the peaceful monotony of the silent past. It heralded in the cacophony that would define the sound of a progressive future.

But many farmers did not fare well. They overextended their purchases of machinery, built homes they could not afford, and continued to be influenced by the ongoing prediction that next year would be better. Near new equipment was resold at bargain prices, and the shrewd farmer would purchase these supplements at auctions and bank foreclosures. Such shrewdness was the character of father and son, Nick and Bill Woronuk. Little by little, with cash purchases only, they increased their farm operation in quantity and quality.

Bill left school when he completed his eighth year. A good student but committed to the farming enterprise, he pursued instead the development of the skills that would serve his chosen industry so well into the future. He became a competent mechanic, welder, plumber, and money manager. With skills developed to the professional trade level, he was able to manage most of his own maintenance, adding to the ability to invest in the farm operation by reducing overhead.

While North America was battling the Depression, Europe was in crisis. Germany, ravaged by impossible demands to repay imposed war debts to the allies, was turning to fascism. Ukraine in the east was ravaged by Russian communism, which imposed a famine, a *holodomor*, that would take many millions of Ukrainian lives. Bukovina, for a time under Rumanian rule, succumbed eventually to the Soviet giant, and Galicia (Halychyna), devastated by Poland, also fell into the communist sphere. Adolph Hitler, a charismatic Austrian, began his seemingly innocuous absorption of countries that were bordering Germany, and the seeds of another war were sown. His ruthless attack on Poland caused an immediate declaration of war from Britain, and the world was in turmoil again.

As soon as Canada declared war on Germany in September 1939, Erena realized the vulnerability of her sons. George had graduated from Normal School, a teacher development program, then common throughout much of the world, and was teaching in the Public School System in Alberta. He was married, and was not a likely candidate for the military. Merose was in high school and yet too young, as was John. But Bill and Alex were of military age, and Erena panicked that they would be required to serve in a European conflict that seemed, to her, to have no bearing on Canada.

The Canadian Government had announced that one son would be permitted to maintain a farm operation, to assure the supply of food for the war effort. Alex immediately volunteered to accept military service and allow Bill to become ineligible for the draft by the one son per farm rule. In 1940, irrespective of his mother's tears, Alex began a five-year military service. He would survive the war physically unimpaired, but suffered a serious, albeit temporary, stress syndrome.

The demand for cereal grains during WWII raised grain prices. Unemployed young men joined the military or were eventually drafted, and farm help was hard to find. The old 15-30 McCormick-Deering tractor was unable to fill the needs of a farm capable of producing substantial quantities of grain. Bill bought a 201 Massey Harris tractor on rubber tires in 1941, the newest and most advanced draft machine of its time. The Massey Harris Company was allowed to produce only a few of these tractors, since the industrial heartland dedicated its production to war materiel. George Lazoruk, son of Nick Lazoruk, also free of military obligation by dedication to the farm operation, purchased a smaller version in the 101 tractor.

Bill enrolled in a brief course at Olds Agricultural College in Olds, Alberta, to learn the fundamentals of the construction of an implement that would replace several men during harvest. With help from George Lazoruk, he built what was to be named a *stook sweep*. Improvised to attach to George's 101 Massey-Harris tractor, it functioned superbly, and indeed did replace several men and teams of horses to bring grain bundles to the threshing machine. While sons in both families suffered through years of war overseas, the ingenuity of such devices as the stook sweep allowed the farm operation to thrive.

Through the war years, Nick Woronuk had concentrated his efforts on gardening, and left the operation of motorized farm equipment in the hands of his son, Bill. Nick never did feel comfortable with motorized equipment; he had become an obsolete farmer. He laughed about it, and he took pride in his son's skills and accomplishments. Merose was soon to graduate in dentistry, George had given up teaching and worked for the American Army as accounting personnel, and then with the war's end, moved to a private car and truck dealership in Grimshaw, Alberta, to open his own General Motors dealership.

Alex returned from the war suffering from the stresses he had endured, took veterans benefits of two quarters of excellent land through the Veteran's Land Act, and attempted to farm along with Bill. But farming had not been, nor was it then, Alex's forte. He rented the land to his brother and joined George in business. In time, as their business prospered, they moved to even more lucrative ventures in transportation. Alex signed the land over to his brother to make the total land holdings substantial and the farm operation a complete success.

During the years immediately following the war, farm machinery in the U.S. was scarce. American farmers were seriously needing help with their harvests, and Canadian farmers, their season significantly later, transported their combines to the southern United States and assisted the Americans with their harvest. In 1947, John left in the middle of his final high school year to accompany Bill on such a venture. It was a highly successful experience and, with the cash resources it offered, Bill was able to purchase yet more land while John used his share to finance a university education leading to a degree in dentistry in the United States.

# FINALE

**N**ick and Erena looked back at their life experience and shook their heads in disbelief. Nick, a humble peasant from Bukovina, and Erena, a daughter of peasants in a neighboring village, without formal education, had together, with spirit and perseverance, created the foundation for prosperity for their children. Their own lives transformed from living in a cave to a modern lifestyle, with most of the conveniences available at the time. And Nick had his youthful dream fulfilled: he owned a hat, spats, and a suitcase.

There was, however, an overcast that obliterated the light that shone on them. In Bukovina, their remaining relatives had paid a price that only ideologies can command. Communism had strangled the economy and freedoms of the peasantry. Invasion by Germany followed; then a final retreat. In each direction it brought about a scorched earth policy. They suffered the atrocities perpetrated by the German armies on one side and the Russian armies on the other. Nick lost his only brother, Simon, along with his three sons who all died in war, and their wives perished in gulags in Siberia. Such familial losses

wore heavily on Nick's conscience. Unable to break through communist bureaucracy to bring his relatives to Canada, the deaths of these
family members troubled Nick the rest of his life.

Nick lived until November of 1956. A diagnosis of probable cancer
took his life, but he had seen his last son John marry earlier that year,
and about to complete his education in dentistry in Oregon. A day
before he passed away Nick told his son John not to grieve; life was
a struggle, and he had won. He was looking forward to a rest. Erena
lived another 35 years to the age of 96. Her mind remained superbly
active and alert and her body strong. Her passion, her Garden of
Eden, was maintained weed free and verdant even beyond her 90th
year. Two of her children predeceased her, however. George passed
away from the stress of a successful business when only 54 years of age,
and Alex followed from the same causes at his age of 56. After their
deaths, Merose passed at 72 and Bill at 93. John and his wife Lorena
are enjoying retirement.

Did Nick and Erena find their Eden? One episode provides light
to that question. In the early 1950s, Nick and Erena's sons wanted to
send their parents on a trip back to Bukovina, to visit the lands and
people they left so many years ago. When the plans were disclosed to
them, Nick responded this way: "Absolutely no! Go back to Bukovina?
Thank God I got out of there. Canada is my home. Don't take me out
of Canada." Erena agreed.

# EPILOGUE

A biographical novel has to end but ending this one is difficult. All members of the original four families about whom this story was told have passed on, their toil completed and their mark made in the loam of the country they chose and loved. Leaving the story there is convenient but it is not an ending. The pioneers' objectives contained a vision of a better life for themselves and their progeny.

In their eyes, the future for them would now be our present. From a perspective of reviewing the past, knowing the present, and looking into the future, it resembles the concept of an endless spiral where there is a beginning but there is no end. For a century the homestead lands selected by Nick Woronuk and Mike Lazoruk for themselves and their families have continued to grow the grain that has satiated the biological needs of countless peoples all over the world. In two of the families, the Woronuk and the Chalus families, the particular homesteads filed on in 1913 still remain with their grandsons bearing the same name a century later.

The intent in this writing was to treat each of the pioneers equally, but that proved impossible. The history of their lives was not equally available: Nick Woronuk wrote a brief biography of his life, as did Mike Lazoruk. Erena Woronuk *recorded several hours with the prompting of her son, Merose. There were the count-less episodes around table-talk that related anecdotes that were not recorded except in memory. In recollecting them, their weight fell naturally on the side of the Woronuks, and so the story falls more on this family than the others. It is not to say that this family was at all more integral to the success of the venture into the Peace River Country than any of the other families. In fact, it is clear that each adult in the original move from Arbakka was critical to the final success of all.*

*Looking back at this venture and having lived a portion of it, I see it as unique. Four families were bound by a Lazoruk member within each, prompted by the impa-tience of one, a brother-in-law, who would seek a land like Eden, and convince the others to follow on an escapade that defies present day imagination. Throughout their lives they lived in harmony despite their diverse personalities. Although the land filtered to a few who chose to farm, the progeny scattered from their nest in Rycroft to help build a foundation for their Canada in fields of business, education, literature, science, health, and technology. It is from this diaspora that relatives and family flocked back to the exact spots in Rycroft where a century before, the original settlers pitched their tents in their Eden.*

*Nick and Erena Woronuk about 1935*

*Woronuk's Aladdin home 1932. Their verdant garden in the foreground*

*Erena Woronuk at age 90*

*Nick Woronuk at age 60*

Printed in Canada